Fiona Dodd, The Big Book

The Authors

Short biographies of the pioneers of the twelve step movement

Fiona Dodd

Fiona Dodd, The Big Book Stories

To Those Who Trudged the Road Before Us

Copyright © 2012 Author Name
All rights reserved.
ISBN: 9798670645867

Table of Contents

Introduction

Original manuscript only...........................1
This story appeared in the original manuscript but was removed before the first edition was printed in April 1939

Del Tyron, "Ace Full-Seven-Eleven" 2

First Edition only...................................3
These stories appeared only in the first edition and were not reuse in the second or third editions

(Hank) Henry P., "The Unbeliever" 4
Florence R., "A Feminine Victory" 6
William R., "A Business Man's Recovery" 7
Harry B., "A Different Slant" 8
Walter B., "The Back-Slider" 10
Ernie G., "The Seventh Month Slip" 12
Tom L., "My Wife and I" 14
William (Bill) V. H., "A Ward of the Probate Court" 16
Charlie S., "Riding the Rods" 18
Bob O., "The Salesman" 20
Wallace (Wally) G., "Fired Again" 22
Paul S., "Truth Freed Me!" 24
Harold S., "Smile With Me, At Me" 26
Henry J. Z., "A Close Shave" 28
Norman H., "Educated Agnostic" 30
Ralph F., "Another Prodigal Story" 32
Myron W., "Hindsight" 34
Horace R. (Popsy) M., "On His Way" 36

Marie B., "An Alcoholic's Wife" 38
Ray C., "An Artist's Concept" 39
Lloyd T., "The Rolling Stone" 41
Pat C., "Lone Endeavor" 43

Second Edition only 45

These new stories (written in 1955) appeared only in the second edition and were not reused in the third edition

John P., "The Professor and the Paradox" 46
Author unknown, "His Conscience" 48
Fred (last name unknown), "New Vision for a Sculptor" 50
Joe M., "Joe's Woes" 53
Bill G., "There's Nothing the Matter With Me!" 56
Annie C., "Annie the Cop Fighter" 58
Nancy F., "The Independent Blonde" 60

Third Edition 63

PIONEERS OF A.A.

Robert H. S., M.D., "The Doctor's Nightmare"
("Doctor Bob's Nightmare" in 2nd/3rd eds.) 64
Bill D., "Alcoholics Anonymous Number Three"
("The Man on the Bed" in 2nd/3rd eds.) 68
Dick S., "The Car Smasher"
("He Had to be Shown" in 2nd ed.) 70
Albert (Abby) G., "He Thought He Could Drink like a Gentleman" 72
Margaret (Marty) M., "Women Suffer Too" 75
Joe D., "The European Drinker" 79
Jim B., "The Vicious Cycle" 82
Jim S., "Traveler, Editor, Scholar"
("The News Hawk" in 2nd/3rd eds.) 85
Ethel M., "From Farm to City" 87

Archie T., "The Fearful One"
("The Man Who Mastered Fear" in 2nd/3rd eds.) 90
Earl T., "He Sold Himself Short" 93
Clarence S., "Home Brewmeister" 96
Sylvia K., "The Keys of the Kingdom" 99

THEY STOPPED IN TIME

Author unknown, "Too Young?" 103
Ceil F., "Fear of Fear" 105
Cecil (Teet) C., "Those Golden Years" 107
Author unknown, "The Housewife Who Drank at Home" 109
Trevor K., Lucknow, India, "Lifesaving Words" 111
Dr. Earle M., "Physician, Heal Thyself!" 113
Lisa, "A Teen-Ager's Decision 117
Pete W., "Rum, Radio and Rebellion" 119
Author unknown, "Any Day Was Washday" 123
Chet R., "It Might Have Been Worse" 125
Esther E., "A Flower of the South" 128
Author unknown, "Calculating the Costs" 131
Felicia G., "Stars Don't Fall" 132
Harris K., "Growing Up All Over Again" 135
Author unknown, "Unto the Second Generation" 137
Author unknown, "Me an Alcoholic?" 140
Dr. Paul O., "Doctor, Alcoholic, Addict"
("Acceptance Was the Answer" in 4th ed.) 142

THEY LOST NEARLY ALL

Morris B., "A Five-Time Loser Wins" 146
Helen B., "Promoted to Chronic" 148
Maynard B., "Join the Tribe" 150
Author unknown, "Belle of the Bar" 152
Jim S., M.D., "Jim's Story" 154
John Henry F. (Fitz) M., "Our Southern Friend" 157

Author unknown, "The Prisoner Freed" 160
Pat M., "Desperation Drinking" 162
Sackville O'C. M., "The Career Officer" 163
Bertha V., "Another Chance" 166
E. B. R. (Bob), "He Who Loses His Life" 167
Wynn C. L., "Freedom From Bondage" 168
Bob P., "A.A. Taught Him to Handle Sobriety" 172

Introduction

The following is a copy of a report on the history of the Big Book that was prepared by the Alcoholics Anonymous World Services staff, and circulated among the Conference, Area and District Literature Committee members, to give them some background as they approached their work on the then-proposed Fourth Edition.

11 Jun 1997

History of Preparation and Publication of the First, Second and Third Editions of the Big Book, Alcoholics Anonymous Prepared by Doug R., A.A.W.S. Staff.

This is an attempt to review the history of the preparation for and publication of the First, Second and Third Editions of the Big Book, Alcoholics Anonymous. The resources of the Archives, the Files Department, the Literature committee records, both Conference and Trustees, as well as memories of present and past staff members at the General Service Office are being used.

First Edition

On a borrowed $4,000 Alcoholics Anonymous was produced, by Works Publishing in 1939. This little company, formed by Bill and Dr. Bob and their non-alcoholic friends along with other founding members was taken over by the Alcoholic Foundation in 1940 when the shareholders and Charles B. Towns were paid off in full by the Foundation for their 'investments' in the project. Thus, our basic text has been held in trust by first, the Foundation, and now A.A. World Services, Inc., for the Society of Alcoholics Anonymous for all time.

In the Foreword to the First Edition, we find the premise, the simple statement of purpose which remains the hub of unity for the Fellowship, "We of Alcoholics Anonymous are more than 100 men and women who have recovered from a seemingly helpless state of mind and body. To show other alcoholics precisely how we have recovered is the main purpose of this book. "(Page iii, Foreword to the First Edition of Big Book, Alcoholics Anonymous.)

In a speech that Bill gave in Fort Worth about the writing of the book, he says,

> I suppose the book yarn really started in the living room of Doc and Annie Smith. As you know, I landed there in the summer of '35, a little group caught hold. I helped Smithy briefly with it and he went on to found the first A.A. group in the world. And, as with all new groups, it was nearly all failure, but now and then, somebody saw the light and there was progress. Pampered, I got back to New York a little more experienced; a group started there, and by the time we got around to 1937, this thinking had leaped a little over into Cleveland, and began to move south into New York. But it was still, we thought in those years, flying blind, a flickering candle indeed, that might at any moment be snuffed out. So, on this late fall afternoon in 1937, Smithy and I were talking together in his living room, Anne sitting there, when we began to count noses. How many people had stayed dry; in Akron, in New York, maybe a few in Cleveland? How many had stayed dry and for how long? And when we added up the total, it sure was a handful of, I don't know, 35, 40 maybe. But enough time had elapsed on enough really fatal cases of alcoholism, so that we grasped the importance of these small statistics.
>
> Bob and I saw for the first time that this thing was going to succeed. That God in his providence and mercy had thrown a new light into the dark coves where we and our kind had been and were still by the millions dwelling. I never can forget the elation and ecstasy that seized us both. And then we sat happily talking and reflecting. We reflected that well, a couple of score of drunks were sober but this had taken three long years. There had been an immense amount of failure and a long time had been taken just to sober up the handful. How

could we transmit our message to them, and by what means ... how could this light be a reflection and transmitted without being distorted and garbled?... And we touched on the book. The group conscience consisted of 18 men good and true ... and the good and true men, you could see right away, were damned skeptical about it all. Almost with one voice, they chorused, 'Let's keep it simple—this is going to bring money into this thing, this is going to create a professional class. We'll all be ruined.' Well, I countered, 'That's a very good argument. Lots to what you say... but even within gunshot of this very house, alcoholics are dying like flies. And if this thing doesn't move any faster than it has in the last three years, it may be another ten before it gets to the outskirts of Akron. How in God's name are we going to carry this message to others? We've got to take some kind of chance. We can't keep it so simple that it becomes anarchy and gets complicated. We can't keep it so simple that it won't propagate itself. And we've got to have a lot of money to do these things.'

The history of the book project is well-documented in Bill's writings. It is a wonderful story which bears repeating again and again because of its significance to the fellowship. The principles which were employed by the early timers and their friends will keep us in good stead as we travel the road to the Fourth Edition of the Big Book.

Second Edition

The progress through to production of the Second Edition of the Big Book is not as nearly as well-documented as the First Edition. We do have a letter from Bill to Bernard Smith in which he notes that he, himself, will do most of the revision. And in the Archives we can see a copy of the Big Book which includes Bill's notes for the Second Edition.

In June 14, 1954, letter to Bernard Smith, Bill wrote:

The story section of the Big Book is far more important than most of us think. It is our principle means of identifying with the reader outside of A.A. It is the written equivalent of hearing speakers at an A.A. meeting; it is our show window of results. To increase the power and variety of this display to the utmost should be, therefore, no routine or hurried job. The best will be none too good. The difference between "good" and "excellent" can be the difference between prolonged misery and recovery, between life and death, for the reader outside A.A.

There were some cautions enumerated by Bill in considering the revision of the Big Book:

The main purpose of the revision is to bring the story section up to date, to portray more adequately a cross section of those who have found help—the audience for the book is people who are coming to Alcoholics Anonymous now. Those who are here have already heard our stories. Since the audience for the book is likely to be newcomers, anything from the point of view of content or style that might offend or alienate those who are not familiar with the program should be carefully eliminated.

There were also some further interesting notes:

Basic Editorial Approaches

1. The desire to reproduce realistic stories should not be overemphasized to the extent of producing an unrealistic book. The stories are not important because they are tape-recorded, they are important because they have something to say about the people who were helped. There should be no shrinking from the job of editing ruthlessly if such editing will preserve the story without the realism.

2. Profanity, even when mild, rarely contributes as much as it detracts. It should be avoided.

3. All minor geographical references should be avoided. (Names of cities, states, etc.)

4. The stories should be "organized" coherently, either in terms of chronology or of the specific points the individual is trying to make.

5. "Selling" or other "gimmicks"—editorial and otherwise—should be avoided the story section is not a popular magazine. The appearance and approach should be straightforward, without frills.

6. Humor should stem from character of the storyteller and of the situations he describes, not be the result of "gags."

7. The end results of the editing should be that the stories will be suitable for reading aloud—at closed meetings, etc.—without embarrassment.

Bill then proceeded to redo the story section, setting it up in three parts:

Section I, reproduction of eight of the original stories, plus four other "graybeards" as he called them.

Section II, consisting of "a dozen stories about milder cases, 'high bottom,' we call them, of which the present story section includes none."

Section III, where Bill included more low bottom stories selected from tape recordings which had been gathered.

Copies of letters which Bill sent out asking people whose stories seemed like a good possibility for the next edition, to sign a release and send it back to him as soon as possible "so we could get our printer going." A copy of the release letter is also enclosed. I found both fascinating in their warmth and ease of communication.

In one letter to an individual who was interested in sending his story to him, Bill writes, "as you are probably aware the stories we need will be of the straight A.A. variety; the kind which would be most effective with the beginner on our program. We are looking for straight personal narratives which describes the drinking history, how the newcomer arrived in Alcoholics Anonymous, how A.A. affected him, and what A.A. has since accomplished for him. For this purpose, we are not, of course, interested in the more advanced or specialized talks, the lecture or spread-eagle oratory type of talk, we can't very well use for this particular purpose."

Another letter from Bill accompanied all the changes planned for the Second Edition of the A.A. book and enumerates these suggested changes with the caveat "Do the new stories afford the best possible variety—do they cover drinking experiences as well as 22 histories could?" And "Do any of the stories or titles contain material that might repel any considerable number of sensitive alcoholic readers? And if so, what changes are suggested?"

He was planning on sending a galley to the July trustees meeting the next month of 1953 and he continues with a reminder to the trustees, "It will be well to remember that the main purpose of the new story section is identification with the new man or woman alcoholic. So, these stories are not necessarily about the very best A.A. members. They were picked because we thought they packed a wallop."

Later that month Bill sends a letter to Ralph Bugli in which he describes his disappointment in the process which he had planned on using. Apparently, using tape recordings and transcribing those had been clumsy at best, and these stories had not communicated well in the written word. There were a lot of

> ... pungent adjectives, slang and sometimes profanity. Some of the titles intensified this condition more. In a meeting such

talk usually goes over because of the background against which it is given. But not so when the recordings are condensed into writing.

In an AA meeting the essential dignity and spirituality of a good member is evident, no matter what he says. His personality is there for all to see and feel. But a condensed tape does not show much of this, especially when the bulk of the tale consists of spectacular drinking episodes ... there isn't enough background showing what the speaker and its environment was before we drank. Neither is there too much evidence to show what he is like now—economically, socially, spiritually. Hence, we see a horrible drunk, now sober, who is glad to be in A.A. because of the fellowship, 24 hour plan, the Higher Power—or God, maybe.

Bill continues,

Readers have to find in the story section individuals like themselves, economically, mentally and socially. Specially, is this true of women. If, in 22 stories, you discover only four or five folks of substance and education and the rest are assorted and spectacular drunks, then many readers can be repelled. the hard-core of A.A., may be 50% consisting of people coming from substantial backgrounds. Therefore it isn't enough to have a lot of categories. This "respectable" category, in particular, has to bear a reasonable relation to the percentage of such people in A. A. Otherwise, we've got another damaging distortion. The extreme low bottom, reading the present stories would surely be attracted. But would your friends and mine have been drawn to A.A. by these 22 case histories, snobbish, maybe.

Nevertheless, AA experience shows that we have to identify with the people on the basis on where they think they are—not where we think they ought to be.

The upshot of this was that half of the speakers had to be interviewed and the material had to be rewritten and a dozen more stories had to be collected. Bill was concerned with the people who had been working on the project and reminded the trustee that these workers should not be given responsibility for the delays. They were following his direction and the responsibility was mainly his because it had been his idea. He winds up with the sentence, "Don't take any of this too seriously—I may still be a fuddy duddy!"

Third Edition

The documentation for the Third Edition is very different from that of the First and Second since our co-founder, Bill, had been immersed in both the preparation and publication of both of those editions. As I mentioned before, the documentation on the First Edition can be found in letters, talks and writings of Bill W. and history on the Second Edition is a little more difficult to track. Along with the Big Book in which Bill made his notes for the Second Edition, there is much original correspondence to be seen of an archival nature.

The Third Edition, however, is almost totally documented through the reports of the Trustees' Literature Committee and the Conference Literature Committee. The first mention of a Third Edition I could uncover is found in a report of the Big Book Subcommittee dated February 4, 1974. Ralph Ahringer, an "in town" member of the trustees' literature committee was the chair of the Big Book Subcommittee and over the next year and a half, he and members of the staff at GSO worked on the project.

In his memo, Ralph reiterated Bill's comments regarding the purpose of revising the story section of the Big Book, Alcoholics Anonymous. From February 1974 and throughout that year, the Big Book Subcommittee worked, and the stories cut from the Second Edition "They Stopped In Time" and from the Second Edition Section "They Nearly Lost It All" were identified fairly early. The possible replacements required a lot of study. The early list included a caution concerning dated expressions and also suggested that all dates that tended to make the stories seem like "ancient history" be omitted or edited, as Bill had done earlier.

In April of 1974 the Conference Literature Committee received an interim report on the work, and in July the Trustees' Literature Subcommittee report included far less detail concerning story names for the new edition. The going seemed to be getting rough at this point, with much work to be done on reviewing the stories submitted. It also mentioned that they were now considering seven Indian stories, a prison story from the Grapevine, a navy story, a young person's story, as well as still looking for a retiree and another Black story. The subcommittee report noted that they were trying to meet a press deadline of December of 1974.

September of 1974 found the Big Book Subcommittee report documenting correspondence among the committee—staff and Ralph Ahringer. The November Trustees' Literature Committee heard in the report of the Big Book Subcommittee that the new stories "will be sent to the Conference Literature Committee for approval and they will not make the current rerun of the book. It will make the next rerun deadline in 18 months."

By the tone of the communication, the project was simply considered an "update" to be included in the next "rerun" of the Big Book which happened every 18 months or so.

In February of 1975 we see Ralph reporting to the committee that the selection of stories was completed and they would be ready for the next "rerun" of the book and would go to the printers in 12 months' time.

Copies of all of the selections were being mailed to the Trustees' and Conference Literature Committees for their comment and approval.

The secretary to the Trustees' Literature Committee and Conference Literature Committee enclosed two more stories with the Conference Literature Committee background material, at the last minute, for their comments and approval.

The staff members' August report noted that the Big Book was with the editor undergoing final editorial changes to go into the next printing of the Big Book and might be at the printers by the November meeting of the literature committee in 1975.

The February 1976 meeting of the Trustees' Literature Committee found the statement: "The Big Book Third Edition will go to the printers soon. No changes have been made from page xxii through page 312. In Parts 2 and 3 seven stories have been deleted and 13 new stories have been added. The Third Edition will be ready later this year."

The 26th General Service Conference Literature Committee received the report and recommended that the delegates take back to their areas a statement to the effect that the Big Book, Alcoholics Anonymous, Third Edition, is not being changed and that only the stories have been updated and some new ones added.

After the publication and release of the Third Edition, at their August of 1976 meeting, the Trustees' Literature Committee heard the committee secretary report that A.A.W.S. had received many letters with favorable comments about the Third Edition of the Big Book, Alcoholics Anonymous.

A press release dated June 1, 1976, briefly reviewed the history of the Big Book, Alcoholics Anonymous and gave a short overview of the Fellowship as well as inviting correspondence.

Subsequently, sharing from AA members regarding "editorial changes" that had been made in the Foreword to the Second Edition in the Third Edition of the Big Book was received. As a result, 1978's General Service Conference produced an Advisory Action that, "In the next printing of Alcoholics Anonymous the Foreword to the Second Edition be included as it was originally published in the Second Edition. Further it was strongly recommended the delegates should be made aware of any changes under consideration in the book Alcoholics Anonymous prior to publication."

The 1989 Conference Literature Committee suggested distributing of Big Book workshop questions to all delegates as part of the commemoration of the 50th Anniversary of the book, Alcoholics Anonymous. The responses were reviewed by the trustees and it was obvious that the areas participating had experience renewed interest in our Big Book.

Fourth Edition

The 1994 Trustees' Literature Committee reviewed requests for a Fourth Edition of the Big Book and suggested a letter be sent to all delegates seeking Fellowship input on a possible 4th Edition of the Big Book.
 The 1995 General Service Conference recommended that "The first 164 pages of the Big Book, Alcoholics Anonymous, the Preface, the Forewords, the Doctor's Opinion, Dr. Bob's Nightmare and the Appendices remain as is."
 That same year the Conference Literature Committee reviewed the report on area responses "Should There Be a Fourth Edition of the Big Book," and concluded there was no need to publish a Fourth Edition of the Big Book at that time.
 The idea of the Fourth Edition went back to the Trustees Literature Committee since there did seem to be some interest in a Fourth Edition, suggesting that they, the trustees, prepare an outline of the proposed content of a Fourth Edition for consideration at the next Conference. This was seen by the 1996 Conference Literature Committee with a request on how to proceed concerning the topic of the Big Book questionnaire and outline. The Conference Literature Committee decided not to proceed with a questionnaire at that time.
 The 1997 Conference Literature Committee received a recommendation from the Trustees' Literature Committee that a draft Fourth Edition of the Big Book, Alcoholics Anonymous, be developed and the Conference Literature Committee agreed and the General Service Conference recommended that: A draft Fourth Edition of the Big Book, Alcoholics Anonymous be developed and a progress report be brought to the 1998 Conference Literature Committee, keeping in mind the 1995 Advisory Action that: The first 164 pages of the Big Book, Alcoholics Anonymous, the

Preface, the Forewords, The Doctor's Opinion, Dr. Bob's Nightmare, and the Appendices remain as is.

A publication of stories dropped from the First, Second and Third Editions of the Big Book, Alcoholics Anonymous, be developed, and a progress report be brought to the 1998 Conference Literature Committee.

Fiona Dodd, The Big Book Stories

Original manuscript only

This story appeared in the original manuscript but was removed before the first edition was printed in April 1939

Ace Full-Seven-Eleven

Del Tryon, Akron, Ohio

Original manuscript p. 62

There are different theories as to why the story was not included in the first edition. Some have suggested that the author became suspicious of Bill Wilson and Hank P. ("The Unbeliever" in the first edition) when Hank set up Works Publishing to raise money to publish the book, with himself as the self-appointed president, and Bill began talking of listing himself as author of the Big Book. Bill would then be entitled to royalties. Others claim that the author wanted to be paid for his story, or to receive a share of the royalties on the book. None of these theories can be verified.

According to his story, he was the son of a pharmacist and studied pharmacy, but before he could take the state board examination he was drafted. In the Army he began gambling and learning to manipulate the dice and cards to his own advantage.

After the war he became a professional gambler. He spent some time in jail, perhaps for gambling or drinking. One source claims it was for bootlegging.

He was hospitalized many times, and eventually his wife had him committed to an insane asylum. He was in and out of the asylum several times. During one of his confinements he met another alcoholic who had lost nearly all. This man had been a hobo and may have been Charlie S. ("Riding the Rods" in the first edition). During his last confinement his friend was not there, but soon he came to visit and to carry the message of A.A.

An agnostic or atheist when he entered, he eventually came to believe in a Divine Father, and that His will was the best bet.

No further information is available.

First Edition only

These stories appeared only in the first edition and were not reused in the second or third editions.

The Unbeliever

Henry (Hank) P., New Jersey

Orig. ms. and 1st ed. p. 194

Hank was the first man Bill W. was successful in sobering up after returning from his famous trip to Akron where he met Dr. Bob. Thus Hank was A.A. No. 2 in New York prior to resuming drinking about four years later. His original date of sobriety was either October or November 1935.

Hank was a salesman, an agnostic, and a former Standard Oil of New Jersey executive, who had lost his job because of drinking. He wound up at Towns Hospital, where Bill found him in the fall of 1935. The first mention of Hank in the Big Book is on page xxix of "The Doctor's Opinion." He is believed to be the man Dr. Silkworth described who seemed to be a case of pathological mental deterioration. (Hank later became very paranoid and Dr. Silkworth warned Bill he might become dangerous.)

When Bill and Lois lost their home on Clinton Street, Brooklyn, it was to Hank P.'s home in New Jersey that they moved for a short time.

He and Jim B. ("The Vicious Cycle"), lead the fight against too much talk of God in the 12 steps, which resulted in the compromise "God as we understood Him."

Hank had a small business, Honor Dealers, in Newark, NJ. It is the little company mentioned on page 149. According to one source, he had conceived it as a way of getting back at Standard Oil, which had fired him. Bill W. and Jim B. worked there for a time and Bill dictated most of the Big Book to Ruth Hock in this office.

Ruth Hock said the Big Book would not have been written without Bill, and it would not have been published without Hank.

And Hank wrote, except for the opening paragraph, the chapter "To Employers."

But Hank became very hostile toward Bill. Problems developed between them over the way Hank was setting up Works Publishing Co., as a for profit corporation, with himself as President. As a result of the feedback from group members, Bill listed himself as the sole author of the Big Book as a means of counter-balancing this.

There were other problems over money, and over Ruth Hock. Hank wanted to divorce his wife, Kathleen, and marry Ruth, and when Ruth decided to go with Bill when he moved the A.A. office out of Honor Dealers, Hank was furious. Bill paid him $200 for the office furniture (which he claimed he still owned, but which had been purchased from him earlier), in exchange for Hank turning over his stock in Works Publishing, as all the others had done. Hank then went to Cleveland to try to start problems for Bill there.

No one knows exactly when Hank had started drinking again, but in the diary Lois W. kept there are various September 1939 entries that mention that Hank was drunk. He did get back on the program for a short time at some later date but it didn't last.

Nevertheless, A.A. owes Hank a debt of gratitude for his many contributions during his all too short period of sobriety.

He died after a long illness at Glenwood Sanitarium in Trenton, New Jersey, on January 18, 1954, at the age of fifty-seven. Lois W. ascribed his death to drinking. Funeral services were held Thursday, January 22 at Blackwell Memorial Home. Rev. A. Kenneth Magner of the First Presbyterian Church performed the service.

At the time of his death he and his wife, Kathleen Nixon P. (whom he had remarried after two failed marriages) were living at Washington-Crossing Road, Pennington, New Jersey. One son, Henry G. P., Jr., was living in Madeira Beach, Florida. A second son Robert S. P., was living in Pennington.

A Feminine Victory

Florence R., New York City

Orig. ms. and 1st ed. p. 217

Florence was the first woman to get sober in A.A., even for a short time. She came to A.A. in New York in March of 1937. She had several slips but was sober over a year when she wrote her story for the Big Book.

It must have been difficult for Florence being the only woman. She prayed for inspiration to tell her story in a manner that would give other women courage to seek the help that she had been given.

She was the ex-wife of a man Bill W. had known on Wall Street. She thought the cause of her drinking would be removed when she and her husband were divorced. But it was her ex-husband who took Lois W. to visit her at Bellevue. Bill and Lois got her out of Bellevue and she stayed in their home for a time. After she left their home, she stayed with other members of the fellowship.

In part, due to Florence having been sober more than a year, "One Hundred Men" was discarded as the name for the Big Book.

She moved to Washington, D.C. and tried to help Fitz M. ("Our Southern Friend"), who after sobering up in New York started A.A. in Washington, D.C. She married an alcoholic she met there, who unfortunately did not get sober. Eventually Florence started drinking again and disappeared. Fitz M. found her in the morgue. She had committed suicide.

Despite her relapse and death from alcoholism, Florence helped pave the way for the many women who followed. She was in Washington by the time Marty M. ("Women Suffer Too"), the next woman to arrive in A.A. in New York, entered the program. Marty only met her once or twice, but her story in the Big Book no doubt encouraged Marty.

A Business Man's Recovery

William R., New Jersey

Orig. ms. and 1st ed. p. 242

Bill R. was born in 1900. According to his story in the Big Book, he first got sober in February 1937.

When the Alcoholic Foundation was established in the spring of 1938, he was appointed as a trustee. He almost immediately got drunk and was replaced by Harry B. ("A Different Slant")

He was underage to join the Army in WW I, but ran away from home and lied about his age to join up. It was in the Army that he started to drink.

He tried many geographic cures. Instead of coming home from Germany after the war he stayed, then took jobs in Russia, England, and back to Germany. He came home in 1924 hoping Prohibition could help him stop drinking. There he discovered the speakeasies. So he shipped off to the Venezuela for a job in the oil fields. They soon poured him on a ship and sent him home.

He had tried doctors, hospitals, psychiatrists, rest cures, changes of scenery, etc., to try to stop drinking. He got married to a woman named Kathleen, hoping marriage would solve his problem. But even Kathleen couldn't help.

Finally he consulted a doctor who referred him to A.A. Bill W. talked to him and told him his own story, then told him to think about it for a few days. He was back to see Bill again the next day.

A Different Slant

Harry B., New York

Orig. ms. and 1st ed. p. 252

His date of sobriety was probably June 1938. It is said that he sued to get the money he had loaned A.A. to get the Big Book published refunded.

Harry was probably an accountant. He is believed to be "Fred, a partner in a well known accounting firm" whose story is told on pages 39 through 43 of the Big Book.

He was happily married with fine children, sufficient income to indulge his whims and future financial security. He was known as a conservative, sound businessman. To all appearances he was a stable, well-balanced individual, with an attractive personality who made friends easily.

However, he missed going to his office several times because of drinking, and when he failed in efforts to stop on his own, had to be hospitalized—a blow to his ego. At the hospital a doctor told him about a group of men staying sober, and he reluctantly consented to have one of them call on him, only to be polite to the doctor. He refused help from the man who called on him, but within sixty days, after leaving the hospital the second time, he was pounding at his door, willing to do anything to conquer the vicious thing that had conquered him.

He soon learned that not only had his drinking problem been relieved, but quite as important was the discovery that spiritual principles would solve all his problems.

While his old way of living was by no means a bad one, he would not go back to it he would not go back to it even if he could. His worst days in the fellowship were better than his best days when he was drinking.

His story is the shortest in the 1st edition. He had only one point he wanted to make. Even a man with everything money can buy, a man with tremendous pride and will power to function in all ordinary circumstances, could become an alcoholic and find himself as hopeless and helpless as the man who has a multitude of worries and troubles. Doctor Earl M. ("Physician Heal Thyself") described this as "the skid row of success," p. 345, 3rd edition.

Harry served on the first board of trustees of the Alcoholic Foundation, replacing Bill R., who got drunk. Soon Harry was drunk, too.

The Back-Slider

Walter B., Cleveland, Ohio

Orig. ms. and 1st ed. p. 265

Walter first joined A.A. in September 1935. He was known as a notorious alcoholic and a regular consumer of paregoric, an over-the-counter opiate then easily available to the general public.

Too young to enlist in World War I, he earned high wages as a machinist, and did very well at his work. He confined his drinking to weekends or occasional parties after work. But he was unsettled and dissatisfied.

He got married, and in 1924 moved to Akron, where he got a job in the largest industrial plant. Things were going well until the stock market crashed and work slowed down. Finally he was laid off.

He found another job that required him to travel. Away from home his drinking increased, and he finally lost that job. A series of jobs followed, but things continued to go down hill.

He was hospitalized several times. During one of his hospitalizations, the chief resident physician, during his rounds, asked him if he would like to stop drinking, and suggested that he send another doctor to see him. This was Dr. Bob.

For two years he stayed sober and his life was greatly improved. Then he started to miss meetings and stopped working the program. He soon started drinking again.

On either August 16 or 18, 1939, he was the first alcoholic admitted by Dr. Bob and Sister Ignatia for the purpose of detoxification. Sister Ignatia labeled his problem as "acute gastritis" in order to admit him. She first put him in a double room. Dr. Bob asked her to move him to a private room so that he could have visitors. No private room being available she moved him to the "flower room," where the nurses watered the flowers that patients had received. The room was also used as a temporary holding room for corpses awaiting transfer to the morgue.

He had probably been in this hospital before under various diagnoses. He talks in his story about many hospitalizations and mentions that in one Catholic hospital, a Sister had talked religion to him and had brought a priest in to see him. They were sorry for him, he said, and assured him he would find relief in Mother Church. He wanted none of it.

When he wrote his story he had been sober about a year and intended to stay close to what he had proven was good for him. Every day he asked God to keep him sober for twenty-four hours. "He has never let me down yet."

His wife, Marie B., wrote the story "An Alcoholic's Wife," which also appears in the 1st edition.

The Seventh Month Slip

Ernie G., Akron, Ohio

Orig. ms. and 1st ed. p. 282

Ernie first got sober in August 1935, probably the first after Bill D. ("A.A. Number 3"), while Bill W. was still staying with Dr. Bob and Anne S. in Akron. He married Dr. Bob's daughter, Sue.

Sue, about 17 at the time, said that the first time she saw Ernie he stopped her on the street to ask her how to get to their house. She pointed out the house, but did not tell him that she was Sue S.

She described him as stout, blue eyed, with reddish hair and a round face. He had a good sense of humor and was a good storyteller, who could make her mother and father laugh, "like nobody I had ever seen, just sitting around the kitchen table, telling stories, and drinking coffee."

He was a wild, devil-may-care young fellow, who had enlisted for a one-year term in the Army when he was only 14 (but could pass for 18). After getting out of the Army he went to Mexico where he worked for an oil company, then rode the range in Texas. He had been married twice and had a son. After returning to Akron he had trouble holding a job because of his drinking.

His parents were very religious and belonged to the same church as T. Henry and Clarace Williams of the Oxford Group. It was probably they who told his parents about how Dr. Bob and Bill W. had found a way to quit drinking.

They urged Ernie to see Dr. Bob and eventually he did. He agreed to be taken to City Hospital where he was tapered off. It took several days, he wrote, for his head to clear and his nerves to settle.

After about six days in the hospital, Dr. Bob, Bill W., and Bill D. visited him and explained their program to him, and he agreed to give it a try. And it worked, he wrote, as long as he allowed it to do so. He stayed sober for about a year and then slipped for seven months.

Finally he went back unshaven, unkempt, looking ill, and bleary-eyed, and asked for help again. He wrote that he was never lectured about his seven-month failure.

Beginning shortly after she finished grade school, Sue had been seeing a boy named Ray Windows. She claims that her parents disapproved of Ray and tried to break them up. Sue believes her father deliberately tried to get her interested in Ernie in order to keep her away from Ray. But it is doubtful that Dr. Bob ever meant for her to become romantically involved with Ernie.

Eventually she broke it off with Ray and married Ernie. He was drunk when he married Sue in September of 1941. Her parents were not aware of the marriage until they heard about it or read it in the papers. They were dismayed.

Dr. Bob said Ernie "never really jelled." Sue S. remembered that they did not know what to do with him. He even got to where he wanted to get paid for speaking at meetings. He had periodic relapses, which got worse and worse until the time he died.

Sue and Ernie had two children, a son (Mickey) and a daughter (Bonna). They divorced about 1965 and she married Ray W. On June 11, 1969, their daughter, Bonna, shot herself, after first killing her six-year old daughter. She was 23 at the time of her death. According to Sue, Ernie never got over it. Bonna died June 11, 1969, and he died two years later to the day, June 11, 1971.

My Wife and I

Tom L., Akron, Ohio

Orig. ms. and 1st ed. p. 287

Tom's first date of sobriety probably was November 1935. (He slipped in December 1937.) His wife, Maybelle, approached Dr. Bob for help.

Tom grew up on a farm and had little education. During and after World War I, he worked in factories for high wages. He married Maybelle, an "able, well-educated woman who had an unusual gift of common sense and far more than the average business vision, a true helpmate in every way."

Together they started a neighborhood grocery store, which prospered, then they bought another. But when the Great Depression hit they lost it. Tom took factory jobs when he could get them, and eventually opened a restaurant. His wife worked with him.

But Tom soon developed a serious drinking problem which eventually caused his wife to confront him and they separated—but for only a week.

They sold their restaurant and Tom took what jobs he could get, but these were hard times. He stayed sober for periods of time because he could not afford the money to drink.

When things improved financially, Tom's drinking got worse. Tom was doing roof repairs and spouting installations, but his wife often had to start the men to work in the morning, do shop jobs, keep the books, and look after the house and family.

Tom became increasingly difficult at home, and Maybelle would quietly ask friends and business associates to drop in casually to talk to him. But they ended up by mildly upbraiding him. When things got truly bad Maybelle left him again, but after a time she returned to try to salvage what she could.

Finally Tom admitted to his wife that he wanted to stop drinking but could not. He asked her for help, and she was eventually referred to Dr. Bob.

Dr. Bob asked if her husband wanted to stop drinking, or was merely temporarily uncomfortable? Had he come to the end of the road? He visited them the following morning, and hospitalized Tom. After a relapse, he and his wife talked it over, and knew it had happened because he had stopped following the program. He acknowledged his fault to God and asked His help to keep to the course he had to follow.

Dr. Bob often called Maybelle for help with the wives of other alcoholics. On one occasion he told her to get hold of Annabelle G., the wife of Wally G. ("Fired Again" in the 1st edition), or her husband would be drunk before he was out of the hospital two hours.

A Ward of the Probate Court

William (Bill) V. H., Akron or Kent, Ohio

Orig. ms. and 1st ed. p. 296

Bill's sobriety date is uncertain. He joined the Fellowship in 1937, and slipped, but was known to be active in the program by September 1937.

Just out of high school Bill landed a job with a local university as an office assistant. He advanced in his work and took a year off to attend an engineering college.

He enlisted in World War I and served on five fronts, from Alsace to the North Sea. When back in the rest area he began drinking red wine and cognac.

When he returned from the war he tried to hide his drinking from his mother and the girl he was to marry, but he got drunk the day their engagement was announced and missed the party. The engagement was off.

He was again working in the President's office at the university, but he also was active in many civic activities. He tried to control his drinking and his sprees were only in private clubs or away from home.

He lost his job at the University although probably not because of his drinking, then held a variety of jobs, and got married, but his marriage failed because of his drinking.

Soon he could not hold a job and began getting arrested for drunk driving and disorderly conduct. Eventually he became a ward of the Probate Court and was admitted to a State hospital at least twice.

Finally, a friend he had known in his drinking days, who was now sober, sought him out and persuaded him to enter the hospital under the care of Dr. Bob.

He was one of the five men Sister Ignatia remembered coming to the hospital after being in terrible accidents because of drinking, who had later come into A.A..

Dr. Bob made a favorable impression on him immediately by spending much time with him telling him of his own drinking experiences.

At the meetings, however, he was not happy with some of the Oxford Group practices. He thought it was throwing the spiritual right at the new person. It was too hard for the alcoholics.

He must have had a friendly, outgoing personality. Dorothy S., then wife of Clarence S. ("The Home Brewmeister") recalled how he had welcomed her when she attended her first meeting the day Clarence got out of the hospital. He told her that he wanted to meet her because they thought Clarence was a pretty wonderful person, and they wanted to see if she was good enough for him.

Bill tried to emulate the humility he saw in Dr. Bob and Anne S. He had twelfth stepped Lavelle K., who with his wife took care of Dr. Bob and Anne in their last years. Lavelle was devastated when Bill slipped, as he had tried to pattern himself on him.

After Dr. Bob and Anne died, Bill hated to go to the meeting at King School (to which the A.A. group had moved). It broke his heart not to see Dr. Bob there, because he had meant so much to him. He said he would go a hell of a long way to hear Dr. Bob.

Riding the Rods

Charlie S., Akron, Ohio

Orig. ms. and 1st ed. p. 303

Charlie probably came to A.A. in May of 1937.

According to his story, when he was fourteen years old, he ran away from the farm where he lived, befriended some hobos, and hoped on a train with two of them headed for Detroit. When they arrived one of them, Tom Casey, took Charlie under his wing, got them both a room with a kindly Irish landlady. Tom looked after Charlie for the next two years, taught him what not to do, made him start a bank account and keep it growing.

Charlie quickly found a job but missed Tom. Soon he started to drink, lost jobs, his bank account dwindled, and disappeared entirely. He was broke and homeless. Soon he was hopping freights again. He found and lost one job after another.

When he tired of city life, he found a job on a farm. Soon he married a young schoolteacher, and needing more money, he moved to an industrial city in Ohio (Akron). He made up his mind to leave liquor behind and get ahead. Soon he had a job, a nice home, and an understanding wife. They had a small circle of friends. He began to try social drinking. But soon he became the bootlegger's first morning customer.

When he finally decided he was just no good and his wife and children would be better off without him he hopped a train for Pittsburgh. After a while he took another back home. He went back to work but continued to have trouble. He tried suicide several times. When he became dangerous, his wife had him placed in a hospital, where he was placed under restraint.

One day he fell into casual conversation with another patient—another alcoholic. They began to compare notes. This man told him of a group of about thirty men who had found a way to stay sober.

He had tried and had stayed sober for a year. He planned to go back to it when he was released from the hospital.

Charlie asked his wife to try to find this group. She was skeptical, but the next day Charlie had a visit from Dr. Bob. When he was released from the hospital, his friend, who had been released a few days earlier, introduced him to several of the other members.

Two years later, when Charlie wrote his story, he said that the way had not been easy, but helping others had strengthened him and helped him to grow. He had obtained a measure of happiness and contentment he had never known before. He knew he would have difficulties every day of his life, but now there was a difference. Now he had a new and tried foundation for every new day.

Charlie may have been the first—but probably not the last—to be twelfth stepped by a relapsed A.A. member.

The Salesman

Bob O., Richfield (Akron), Ohio

Orig. ms. and 1st ed. p. 317

Bob entered the program in December of 1936, but after six months had a slip. He stopped drinking again in May 1937.

His teenage years were uneventful. He was raised on a farm but wanted to be a businessman, so he took a business college course. His first business was buying produce from the family farm and selling it to customers in the city. The business theory he had learned in college helped him to become successful and he soon expanded his business. But in 1921, during an economic slump, he was wiped out. With more time on his hands, his drinking increased.

He worked at a variety of jobs from then on, but most often as a salesman—a career at which he was very good.

He started drinking during Prohibition, and it soon became a habit.

Bob at one time brewed beer at home. He tells how, when a fire threatened to destroy his home, he rushed to the cellar and rescued a keg of wine and all the beer he could carry. He became indignant when his wife suggested that he had better get some of the needed effects out of the house before it burned down.

He lost jobs and his home, and a car accident once put him in the hospital. When he got out of the hospital, he stayed sober for six weeks and had made up his mind to quit but returned to the same pattern.

His marriage deteriorated and his wife divorced him. He had no friends left. His mother tried to help and sent clergymen to talk to him. When his mother heard about Dr. Bob she persuaded him to go with her to see him.

Dr. Bob suggested he be hospitalized for a short time, but he refused. He did agree, however, to go to a meeting. He was as good as his word and met the small group. He liked the informality of the meeting, but the meeting did not impress him. However, he saw men he had known as drinkers apparently staying sober.

It was another six months, after a binge, before, in a maudlin and helpless state, he made his way back to see Dr. Bob.

There was no overnight change in Bob, but he began to enjoy the meetings, and to exchange the drinking habit for something that has helped him in every way. Every morning he read a part of the Bible and asked God to carry him through the day safely. It also helped that Dr. Bob immediately put him to work helping another alcoholic who was hospitalized. All he had to do was tell his story to the new man.

He reunited with his wife, began making good in business and paying off his debts. His former friends and employers were amazed.

He was sober several years when he wrote his story, kept that way, he explained, by submitting his natural will to a Higher Power. He did that on a daily basis.

Fired Again

Wallace (Wally) G., Akron, Ohio

Orig. ms. and 1st ed. p. 325

Wally probably first entered A.A. in May of 1937, but one source says October 1938. But after several years he slipped and had a hard time getting back.

He was an engineer. He must have been handsome; one Akron member described him as having iron-gray hair and looking like President Warren Harding.

He described himself as a man of extremes. When he learned to dance, he had to go dancing every night; when he worked or studied, he wanted no interruptions; and of course, when he drank he could never stop until he was drunk. He started getting drunk before he was sixteen.

Wally must have been a good worker because he rarely had a problem finding a job, and often was rehired by the same company and given another chance. But he was fired again and again. He was once fired from the WPA (Works Progress Administration, a Federal job program instituted during the Depression of the 1930s.)

He was irritated by efforts to help him. His family once persuaded him to enter a sanitarium for thirty days. He left with the firm resolve never to drink again.

Before he left the sanitarium, he answered an advertisement for an engineer in Akron and after an interview, got the job. In about three months he was out of a job again.

Finally, a neighbor, who had heard of Dr. Bob's work, told his wife, Annabelle, about it and she went to see Dr. Bob. Soon Wally was hospitalized by Dr. Bob and began his recovery. About twenty men called on him while he was still in the hospital. He knew five of them, three of whom he had never before seen completely sober.

Annabelle was at first was hard to convince that the program would work, because Wally once brought home an A.A. member he had met in a bar. This was Paul S. ("Truth Freed Me!") during his slip in early 1936. Then her own doctor urged her to see Dr. Bob. Finally, her clergyman, J. C. Wright, got a woman to talk to Annabelle and then made an appointment for her with Dr. Bob. This was probably the neighbor Wally talks about in his story.

Dr. Bob called Maybelle L., wife of Tom L. ("My Wife and I") and told her to get hold of Annabelle or her husband would be drunk before he was out of the hospital two hours. Finally Annabelle took Maybelle's advice and let go and let God. Anne S. also took her under her wing.

After his recovery, Wally and Annabelle took many alcoholics into their home. According to Bill W., they had more success with people they took into their home than did Dr. Bob and Anne S. or Bill and Lois W.

Wally was Dr. Bob's right hand man for many years, and when he eventually slipped everyone was shocked. He had seemed to be doing everything right and working very hard.

Wally had been very hard on those who slipped and wanted to kick them out, which may explain why it took him a long time to get back, but Annabelle dragged him to meetings. He finally got sober again and stayed sober until his death. His attitude toward those who slip, however, changed.

Truth Freed Me!

Paul S., Akron, Ohio

Orig. ms. and 1st ed. p. 336

He knew Dr. Bob prior to joining AA. Dr. Bob formed the habit of stopping at his house for coffee after office hours on Tuesdays and Thursdays. At first, his topic was honesty, and after several trips he suggested Paul stop kidding himself. Then the topic changed to faith—faith in God.

Though he had stopped drinking, he was unable at first to grasp the spiritual program. He was doubtful, fearful, full of self-pity, afraid to humiliate himself. This lasted until December 11th, when he was faced with the absolute necessity of raising a sum of money. He approached a banker and told him the whole story. He believed his need was money, but the banker told him he knew something of what he was trying to do, and believed he was on the right track. He told Paul that if he were right with God, he would do all he could to help him secure the loan.

Paul had found reality. His needs were met from another entirely unexpected source. He was profoundly grateful for the opportunities he had had of seeing and knowing *truth*.

In February of 1937 he brought his brother Dick S. ("The Car Smasher") into the program.

Paul did a lot of twelfth step work. He told one prospect, who complained that he had no job, that he indeed had a job—it was to stay sober and work at this program. That is a full-time job by itself. And he is known to have visited Clarence S. ("The Home Brewmeister") often during his hospital stay.

Paul was close to Dr. Bob and went with him to New York for the Rockefeller dinner on February 8, 1940. And it was Paul who convinced Frank Amos (who was sent to Akron by John D. Rockefeller, Jr., investigate A.A.) that Dr. Bob needed financial help or would have to give up his work with alcoholics. Mr. Amos reported that Paul said it would be criminal to lose Dr. Bob as their leader and suggested that Mr. Rockefeller confidentially arrange for a monthly remuneration for Dr. Bob for a period of at least two years. Paul also got Dr. Bob's son, "Smitty," a job in Cleveland working as a service manager for a tire dealer, after he returned from military service in WW II.

It was Dick S. who was known as "The Car Smasher." But sadly, it was Paul S. who died from a car accident on September 19, 1953. Both brothers remained sober until their deaths.

Smile With Me, At Me

Harold S., Brooklyn, New York

Orig. ms. and 1st ed. p. 340

Harold was an early New York member. He probably stopped drinking in February of 1938 but slipped in June of that year.

Through his long drinking career, he held many and various jobs. He was an accomplished violinist who had played with some well-known orchestras, a radio engineer, a ballet master, and hairdresser. At the time he enlisted in the Navy during World War I, he was working as a host at a celebrated restaurant and cabaret. Having been a radio operator in the navy, he soon became interested in amateur radio. He got a federal license and made a transmitting radio set. Broadcasting radio was just in its infancy then, so he began to make small receiving sets for his friends and neighbors. Finally, he worked up quite a business and opened a store, then two stores, with eleven people working for him. However, within three years' time he had lost both stores, probably in large part due to his drinking.

He drifted from one job to another, peddled brushes, did odd jobs such as painting, and finally got established with a well known piano company as assistant service manager. But when the stock market crashed in 1929 he lost that job. He worked for one of his old competitors who owned a radio store, until his drinking got so bad and he was in such poor physical condition that he had to quit.

His family was concerned about his drinking. His wife had to go to work and, so that they would have someone to care for his son, they moved in with his parents.

His wife contacted a well-known psychiatrist and Harold saw him for a few months. He doctor advised hospitalization from three months to a year, Harold knew he would just go back to drinking as soon as he was released.

What he thought and wanted at the time was "not to want to want to take a drink." He knew it could only be done by himself, but how? After going to as many as six or eight other doctors, some of his own friends advised his wife to make her plans for the future as he was a hopeless case, had no backbone, no will power, and would end up in the gutter.

Finally, his father, a physician, put him in a private New York hospital (probably Towns). When he was there ten days a new friend, "a true friend," asked if he really wanted to stop drinking. And if he did, would he do anything no matter what it was? The program was explained to him, and he met the other members.

After about fourteen weeks, he took the first drink. It took him several tries to get back, but he realized that there was something that he failed to do in those simple steps. He had slipped away from quite a few of some of the most important things he needed to do in order to keep sober.

One morning, after a sleepless night worrying, he turned to the Bible and found help. He returned to the group and began to turn his life over to the care of God.

For a time during 1939, meetings were held in his home.

A Close Shave

Harry D. Z., Orrville, Ohio (suburb of Akron)

Orig. ms. and 1st ed. p. 348

Harry found sobriety in March of 1937, but he may have entered the fellowship as early as January 1937.

He was born in 1890, the youngest of five sons to a "fine Christian mother, and a hard working blacksmith father."

At the age of eight he began tasting his father's beer, and by fourteen, when he quit school, he was drinking wine and hard cider.

He worked as a barber, and acquired several lucrative shops, some with poolrooms and restaurants attached. He married in 1910, during the time he was running his own shops, and fathered ten children.

But the time came when he could no longer finance his own business, so he began to float about the country, working at various jobs, but invariably getting fired in a short time because of his unreliability. His children were usually desperately in need because he spent his money for drinking instead of providing for them.

He finally secured a job in a shop in a small town near Akron. His reputation for drinking soon became more or less generally known, and he was irritated by a deacon and the pastor of a church who, when they were in the shop, constantly invited him to church and Bible classes. He earnestly wished they would mind their own business. But he became friendly with these men, and at last they persuaded him to go to Akron and talk with Dr. Bob.

He listened to Dr. Bob for two hours, and although his mind was quite foggy, he retained a good deal of what was said. He felt that the combined effort of these three Christian gentlemen made it possible for him to have a vital spiritual experience.

That was in March 1937. At the time he wrote his story, he had not had a drink since. He had regained the love of his family and the respect of the community and said the past few years had been the happiest of my life, spent helping others who were afflicted with alcoholism.

He died on December 10, 1960.

Educated Agnostic

Norman H., Darien, Connecticut

Orig. ms. and 1st ed. p. 351

Norman's date of sobriety is uncertain. One source says it was February 1938, another says June 1938.

He had been hospitalized four times. The first three times he left the hospital determined never to drink again. Now, on his fourth visit, he told the kindly doctor (perhaps Dr. Silkworth) that he was a thoroughly hopeless case and would probably continue to return as long as he could beg, borrow, or steal the money to get in.

On the second day in the hospital the doctor told him that he knew of a way he could stop drinking forever. On the third day a man came to talk with him. He talked about alcoholism and a spiritual way of life.

Norman was deeply impressed by his seriousness, but nothing that he said made sense to him. He spoke about God, and Norman did not believe in a God. It was not for him. War, illness, cruelty, stupidity, poverty and greed were not and could not be the product of any purposeful creation.

The next day another man visited him. He, too, was an alcoholic who no longer drank. This second man had not had a drink in over three years. This was probably Fitz M. ("Our Southern Friend") or Hank P. ("The Unbeliever").

He told him of other men who had found sobriety through the recognition of some power beyond themselves and invited him to a meeting on the following Tuesday at Bill W.'s home in Brooklyn.

He told his wife about this group, and she thought he was mentally unbalanced. But she had met this kindly doctor and, since he recommended it, she was willing for him to try it.

The following Tuesday, hardly daring to hope and fearful of the worst, he and his wife attended their first meeting. He had never been so inspired.

That was, for him, the beginning of a new life. Almost imperceptibly he began to change. In the process of this change, he recognized two immensely significant steps for him. He admitted to himself for the first time that all his previous thinking might be wrong, and he consciously wished to believe.

In his story, Norman ends by addressing himself directly to atheists or agnostics, who might read the book. He assured them that their questions had been in his mind also. He could see no satisfactory solution to any of them. But he kept hard to the only thing that seemed to hold out any hope, and gradually his difficulties were lessened. He said he had not given up his intellect for the sake of his soul, nor had he destroyed his integrity to preserve his health and sanity. "All I had feared to lose I have gained and all I feared to gain I have lost."

As a result of this experience, he was convinced that to seek is to find, to ask is to be given. The day never passed that he did not silently cry out in thankfulness, not merely for his release from alcohol, but even more for a change that had given his life new meaning, dignity, and beauty.

Another Prodigal Story

Roland Arthur "Bob" F., Springfield, Massachusetts

Orig. ms. and 1st ed. p. 357

Recent research shows that the author of this story was probably Roland Arthur F. (1882-1946) from Springfield, Massachusetts (who was somewhat confusingly nicknamed "Bob," so his name is sometimes incorrectly given in A.A. documents as Robert). And to add to the confusion, earlier A.A. historians sometimes identified the author of this story as another man with the same last name, Ralph F. (1891-1966) of Pittsfield, Massachusetts. But Ralph's only daughter Eloise was born in February 1911, and the author of this story had a daughter who (he said) was born in June.

Bob had his last drink on June 6, 1938.

He begins by telling of his last drunk. He and a man he met at the bar planned how they would convince his wife that he had been about to commit suicide and how his new friend had saved his life, so that she would be sympathetic rather than angry at his drunken state. When the man started playing with a gun, Ralph got nervous and ran away.

Only the day before he had been in an accident. A Good Samaritan saw his condition and got him away quickly, before the police came, and drove him home. He was dreadfully drunk that day and his wife consulted a lawyer as preliminary to entering a divorce action. He swore to her that he wouldn't drink again and within 24 hours, he was dead drunk.

Several months previously he had spent a week in a New York hospital for alcoholics and came out feeling that everything would be all right, but soon began drinking again.

The next morning was June 7th. He remembered the date because the day before was his daughter's birthday. And that, by the grace of God, was his last spree.

His wife, who had threatened to leave him, ordered him to get dressed because she was taking him to New York to the hospital.

His wife pleaded with the doctor to please do something to save her husband, to save her home, to save their business, and their self-respect.

The doctor assured them that he had something for him this time that would work.

Four days later a man called on him who stated that he, too, had been there several times but had now found relief. That night another man came. He, too, had been released from alcohol. Then the next day a man came, and in a halting but effective way, told how he had placed himself in God's hand and keeping. Almost before Ralph knew it, he was asking God to help him.

Some alcoholics feel a strong resentment against such a spiritual approach. But Ralph was ripe for it.

The following day was Monday and one of these men insisted that Ralph check out from the hospital and go with him to his home in New Jersey. (This may have been Hank P.) He did, and the next night he was taken to a meeting at Bill W.'s home in Brooklyn, where there were more than 30 men like him.

When he returned home, life was very different. He paid off the old debts, had money enough for decent clothes and some to use in helping others. He also worked hard for A.A. He is believed to have started the group in Darien, Connecticut, and at the time he wrote his story there were four in that group. He also may have been the Ralph who worked in the pressroom at A.A.'s second International Convention in St. Louis in July of 1955.

This prodigal had come home.

Hindsight

Myron W., New York City

Orig. ms. and 1st ed. p. 370

Myron sobered up in April of 1936.

His is another story that could have been titled, "Fired Again." He was fired repeatedly, but often could find a still better job. During the Great Depression he was making $10,000 a year—an enormous salary at that time.

He would stop drinking for weeks or even months, then begin to drink moderately. He could do that for a time, but soon he would be back to problem drinking. How many times this happened, he didn't know and didn't even want to know.

His story could also have been called "The Car Smasher." During this period, he completely smashed nine new automobiles, but escaped without injury to himself. Even this, he said, didn't convince him that there might be a God who was looking out for him, perhaps in answer to the prayers of others.

He abused his friends; he didn't want to, but when it was a question of a friendship or a drink, he usually took the drink.

In a final effort to escape he moved to New York, thinking he could leave his reputation and troubles behind him. He was hired by eight nationally known organizations and fired just as quickly when they had checked his references. He felt the world was against him. They wouldn't give him a chance. So, he continued his drinking and took any mediocre job he could get.

He visited churches occasionally, hoping to find something that would help him. On one of these visits, he met a girl he thought could be the answer to all of his problems. He was honest with her about his problems, but she knew better than to marry a man thinking she could reform him. She suggested prayer instead. And she told him "You must be decent for your own sake. And because you want to be decent, not because someone else wants you to be." Myron then started bargaining with God but found that God didn't work that way. He got neither the girl nor his old job back.

Six months later he was sitting in a small hotel, full of remorse and desperate. A middle-aged man approached him and said, "Do you really want to stop drinking?" When he answered yes, the man wrote down a name and address. "When you are sure you do, go and see this man." He walked away. Myron tucked the address into his pocket along with a nickel for subway fare, just in case he ever decided to really quit.

A week later he found himself in the presence of the man whose address was in his pocket. His story was incredible. Myron couldn't believe it, but he had the proof. He met other men whose stories convinced him that in the ranks of men who had been heavy drinkers he was an amateur and a sissy. What he heard was hard to believe but he wanted to believe it and wanted to try it to see if it would work for him. It worked.

He was reconciled to the fact that he might have to wash dishes, scrub floors, or do some menial task for many years in order to re-establish himself as a sober, sane, and reliable person. Although he still wanted and hoped for the better things in life, he was prepared to accept whatever was due him.

Good things began to happen to him. He applied for a position with a national organization. When asked why he had left a previous job, he told the truth. He had been fired for being a drunk. He got the job.

He was sober three and a half years when he wrote his story. Those years were the happiest of his life. He had married a woman who cared enough for him to tell him the nasty truth when he needed to hear it.

He continued to receive obstacles of various kinds. He failed at business at least twenty times. But he was not discouraged, sad or resentful. He knew that only good would come from the experience.

On His Way

Horace R. (Popsy) M., New York City

1st ed. p. 375

Popsy entered A.A. in September of 1938.

He was described as a charming Virginia gentleman. His wife, Sandy, had been a nurse. They lived in a fashionable home on exclusive Sutton Place in Manhattan.

According to his story he was drinking heavily by the age of fifteen and sixteen. Then he decided to leave school. The next few years were spent in civil engineering work, travel, sports, and idleness, and he seemed not to have serious difficulties because of his drinking.

By the time he married and sailed for France during World War I, alcohol had begun to play a big part in his life. Soon he knew he was an alcoholic but would admit it to no one.

Sometime after he was divorced from his first wife, he stopped being a social drinker and became a periodic drunkard, with sprees lasting from three days to three weeks, and the dry intervals lasting from three weeks to four months.

He married again by the age of thirty-five and had a beautiful home. He had a kind, understanding, lovely wife; a partnership in a firm he had helped to found years before; a more than comfortable income; many luxuries and friends; opportunity to follow his interests and hobbies; a love of his work; pride in his success; great health; optimism; and hope.

But he had a growing, gnawing fear about his drinking. Soon he slipped to the bottom, sleeping in cheap hotels, flop houses, police stations and once in a doorway. (Since they appear to have been a wealthy family, this may have been because his wife had kicked him out, or he didn't quite make it home due to his condition.)

He was sent many times to the alcoholic ward of a hospital. Sometimes he could pull himself together and work, but not for long. He became helpless, hopeless, bitter.

When he finally found A.A., he found that his intelligence, instead of drawing him further away from spiritual faith, brought him closer to it. He was finally able to see that God could do an eminently more capable job of running the universe than he. At last, he believed he was on his way.

It was Popsy and his wife who took Marty M. ("Women Suffer Too") to her first meeting, on April 15, 1939. His sister-in-law had given the manuscript of the Big Book to Dr. Tiebout. Marty was a patient of Dr. Tiebout at Blythewood. Dr. Tiebout handed her a card with an address and told her to take the five o'clock train into New York, grab a cab, and go to the address on the card. These people would take her to a meeting. Marty was astounded to find this charming older couple, in this elegant home. Sandy put Marty immediately at ease. They had also invited for dinner a handsome, curly-black-haired, blue-eyed young A.A. Irish man named Brian as Marty's escort for the evening. They had an elegant dinner, after which the four of them caught the subway to Brooklyn across the East River.

An Alcoholic's Wife

Marie B., Cleveland, Ohio

1st ed. p. 378

Marie, a non-alcoholic, was the wife of Walter B. ("The Backslider"). Walter first joined A.A. in September 1935.

There is indication in the Akron archives that Marie may have written the first draft of "To Wives," which Bill then edited. But *Dr. Bob and the Good Oldtimers* and *Lois Remembers* both state that Bill W. wrote it.

She started her brief story by saying "I have the misfortune, or I should say the good fortune, of being an alcoholic's wife. I say misfortune because of the worry and grief that goes with drinking, and good fortune because we found a new way of living."

Marie worried constantly about her husband's drinking, went to work to pay the bills, covered his bad checks, and took care of their home and their son.

When he stopped drinking, she thought their problems were over, but soon found she had to work on her own defects and that they both had to give their problems to God.

She ended her story by saying "My husband and I now talk over our problems and trust in a Divine Power. We have now started to live. When we live with God we want for nothing."

An Artist's Concept

Ray C., New York City

1st ed. p. 380

Ray joined the fellowship in February 1938.

He began his story with a famous quotation: "There is a principle which is a bar against all information, which is proof against all arguments and which cannot fail to keep a man in everlasting ignorance—that principle is contempt prior to investigation."

Ray incorrectly attributed this quotation to Herbert Spencer (1820-1903), as did a number of other books from the 1930s, 40s, and 50s. In fact, it came from a line in William Paley's *A View of the Evidences of Christianity* (1794), as modified by William H. Poole in a book called *Anglo-Israel* (1879).

Ray said that the quotation is descriptive of the mental attitudes of many alcoholics when the subject of religion, as a cure, is first brought to their attention. "It is only when a man has tried everything else, when in utter desperation and terrific need he turns to something bigger than himself, that he gets a glimpse of the way out. It is then that contempt is replaced by hope and hope by fulfillment."

Ray chose to write of his search for spiritual help rather than "a description of the neurotic drinking that made the search necessary."

After investigating his alcoholic problem from every angle, medicine, psychology, psychiatry, and psychoanalysis, he began "flirting" with religion as a possible way out. He had been approaching God intellectually. That only added to his desperation, but a seed had been planted.

Finally, he met a man, probably Bill W., who had for five years "devoted a great deal of time and energy to helping alcoholics." The man told him little he didn't already know, "but what he did have to say was bereft of all fancy spiritual phraseology—it was simple Christianity imparted with Divine Power."

The next day he met over twenty men who "had achieved a mental rebirth from alcoholism." He liked them because they were ordinary men who were not pious nor "holier than thou." He notes that these men were but instruments. "Of themselves they were nothing."

He liked to include notable quotations, not only the Paley/Poole quote, but also a version of Henry David Thoreau's line in *Walden* (1854), which he gives as: "Most men lead lives of quiet desperation." (The famous New England Transcendentalist author actually said, "the mass of men" in *Walden* instead of "most men," so this quotation too is not quite correct.)

It was Ray, a recognized artist, who was asked to design the dust jacket for the first edition of the Big Book. He submitted various designs for consideration including one that was blue and in an Art Deco style. The one chosen was red and yellow, with a little black and a little white. The words Alcoholics Anonymous were printed across the top in large white script. It became known as the circus jacket because of its loud circus colors. The unused blue jacket is today in the Archives at the Stepping Stones Foundation.

His story was not included in the second edition of the Big Book but the Paley/Poole quote (still attributed to Spencer) was placed in the back of the book in Appendix II, "Spiritual Experience."

The Rolling Stone

Lloyd T., Cleveland, Ohio

1st ed. p. 386

Lloyd's date of sobriety is uncertain. One source says it was February of 1937, another says November 1937.

He came from a broken home, and when his parents separated his father went west and became fairly successful. Then it was decided that Lloyd should go to a preparatory school in Chicago. Soon he was in trouble in school and his father sent him money to join him in the West.

It was a lonely time for Lloyd, as his father was away most of the day and spent evenings reading and studying religious books. Lloyd became very hostile toward religion, and that lasted for years.

When he was fourteen, but looked eighteen, he started hanging out in saloons. On vacation his father let him go alone to San Francisco. While there he decided he wanted to see the world and signed on as an apprentice on a ship.

He developed into a steady drinker and, when going to sea, took enough liquor along to last for the trip. At foreign ports if American liquor was not available or cost too much he tried the native drinks, which were often very potent.

He visited most of the ports in the world, stayed in some of them for some time, and every place he went he found alcoholic beverages available.

At twenty he stopped going to sea, and eventually got into the building trade. He made good money, but never stayed in one place for very long, ever the "rolling stone."

When World War I started he was twenty-nine and living in Texas. When he left Texas, he learned that the train would be stopping in his hometown for an hour. He saw his mother very briefly for the first time in eleven years. He promised her that after the war he would come home.

He tried to stop drinking but could not. There were many visits to doctors and sanitariums. He was then his mother's sole support, and he caused his mother much misery.

Finally, he heard about Doctor Bob in Akron, and went to see him. Dr. Bob put him in the hospital and told him that unless he was sincere in wanting to quit, he was just wasting their time. But Lloyd was willing to do anything. Eventually he had a religious awakening.

He was active in twelfth step work and it was his name and address that Dr. Bob gave Dorothy S., then married to Clarence S. ("The Home Brewmeister"), when she appealed to him for help for her husband. Lloyd became Clarence's sponsor. But when Clarence announced that he was starting a meeting in Cleveland which would be called Alcoholics Anonymous, Lloyd stayed with the Oxford Group, at least until the Akron group also broke away.

He was fifty years old when he wrote his story, and unmarried. But he had become sane and sensible again, had made his mother happy and made many new friends. He had gained the respect of his fellow men and learned how to enjoy life. He had been sober nearly a year and a half when he wrote his story.

Lone Endeavor

Pat C., Los Angeles, California

1st edition 1st printing p. 391;
removed from 2nd printing

Pat first stopped drinking in January 1939.

Bill W., Ruth Hock, and Hank P. were sending copies of the manuscript around the country to friends for comment. A copy reached the hands of Pat's mother, and Pat read it. He then arranged to be hospitalized for detoxification "to get the liquor out of my system and start the new idea right."

On about February 27, 1939, six weeks after leaving the hospital on January 15, 1939, he wrote a letter to The Alcoholic Foundation in New York saying he had recovered.

He thanked them for the draft of the book which he had read cover to cover. He told them how he had started drinking in 1917, about his service in World War I, how his drinking continued in France and after he got back home from the war. The following fifteen years were "one drunk after another."

He enlisted in the Marine Corps. At first he drank very little and was promoted to Gunnery Sergeant. But he started drinking heavily again and was reduced in rank, then sent to China (which didn't help his drinking problem any). He did not reenlist.

After he returned, his wife left him because of his drinking, and he couldn't hold a job. He married again, but his wife and mother were worried about his drinking.

Then he told how his mother had heard of A.A in an article published by a doctor and had written the doctor for information. He turned the letter over to A.A., which, of course, had immediately responded.

Pat's letter said he was already reaching out to help other alcoholics.

So, they sent him a wire asking his permission to use the letter anonymously in the book, as the first example of what might be accomplished without personal contact. He wired back the next day: "Permission granted with pleasure. Lots of Luck."

This was the first time anyone had sobered up just from reading the book, so everyone was very excited. After the exchange of correspondence, which appears in the first edition, a collection was taken up to buy a bus ticket to bring him to New York.

When the bus showed up in New York, a man fitting his given description did *not* exit the vehicle. Confused, the welcoming party asked the driver if he had seen a man of the description aboard the bus at any time. He replied that the man was sleeping it off *under* the back seat! So, the story was removed from the second printing of the Big Book.

In the Mid-Southern California Area 9 Archives is a letter from Kaye Miller, a non-alcoholic who started the first A.A. meeting in Los Angeles, to Bill W. in New York. Bill had asked her to put on paper her early recollection of A.A. in Southern California. He also asked about Pat C. In this 1944 letter she writes that Pat was attending meetings again and had been sober about a year.

The story was ghost written by Ruth Hock, Bill W.'s secretary, from correspondence between the New York office and Pat and his mother.

Second Edition only

These new stories (written in 1955) appeared only in the second edition and were not reused in the third edition

The Professor and the Paradox

John P., Tuscaloosa, Alabama

2nd ed. p. 336

"Says he, 'We A.A.s surrender to win; we give away to keep; we suffer to get well; and we die to live.'"

According to a talk John gave on Founders Day 1978 in Akron, he entered A.A. in February of 1949.

He was born in Atlanta, Georgia, and had a thick southern accent. He described himself as having always been shy, sensitive, fearful, envious, and resentful, which in turn lead him to be arrogantly independent, a defiant personality. He believed he got his Ph.D. degree principally because he wanted to either outdo or defy everybody else. He published a great deal of scholarly research, perhaps for the same reason.

He finished graduate school at the age of 30, and taught English at the University of Alabama for 21 years. That is where he was working when he entered A.A. He later taught at Kent State University in Ohio. (He joked in a talk he gave in 1978 about teaching Shakespeare with a southern accent, and having taught freshman English to Jim Nabors, television's Gomer Pyle. Had he known Nabors was going to make so much money, he would have sat in Nabors' seat and let Nabors teach the class.)

He began as a social drinker, in his early twenties, and did not experience any problems with drinking until well after he finished graduate school. But as the tensions and anxieties of his life mounted, and the setbacks from perfection began to increase, he "slipped over the line between moderate drinking and alcoholism."

John said, "there are all kinds of drunks: melancholy drunks, weeping drunks, traveling drunks, slap-happy and stupid drunks, and a number of other varieties." He was a self-aggrandizing and occasionally violent drunk.

His crises came when, during a drunk, he became "violently insane" and landed in the City Jail. Soon after he was ready for A.A.

John gave very humorous talks. For example, he said in his 1978 talk that he did not know why his story was removed from the third edition, perhaps the New York office thought he had died.

He also joked about how having your story in the Big Book could sometimes cause problems. He told how after he had talked at a state A.A. convention in Little Rock, Arkansas, he overheard a man say that he was a fake, a liar, and a thief. The man thought he had stolen every word of his story out of a story in the Big Book which the man had just read the night before.

He discusses four paradoxes in his story. A paradox, he explains, is a statement seemingly self-contradictory; a statement which appears to be false, but which, upon careful examination, in certain instances proves to be true. The four paradoxes are, (1) we surrender to win, (2) we give away to keep, (3) we suffer to get well and (4) we die to live.

John updated his story for the January 1968 *A.A. Grapevine*. In the update he said that in A.A. we don't just quit drinking. "We learn to change our self-centeredness, to stop running away from things we don't like, and to remove or at least adjust our emotional shortcomings. We do these things by taking seriously and honestly our Twelve Steps, the nearest thing to a 'cure' for alcoholism that anybody has yet discovered. We learn to do these things not by just memorizing the Steps (though that is a good idea), but by attempting to live and act them each day of our lives. And eventually, often when we least expect it, we discover that as a result of all this we are happy and contented and full of thanksgiving—something I once knew (or thought I knew) I could never be, without drinking."

His Conscience

Author unknown, Canada

2nd ed. p. 365

"It was the only part of him that was soluble in alcohol."

It is believed that this author first got sober in 1938.

He came from a family of five children and had a very happy childhood in a small Canadian town. His parents were religious, without over emphasizing it.

He never drank until he joined the Army in World War I and drank very little while in the service. In France he gave his rum ration away far more often than he drank it.

He was sent back to Canada in the middle of the war because he was wounded and suffering from shock. He did some drinking with friends while waiting for his final discharge papers, but out of the Army he only had a drink or two on special occasions, two or three times a year. That continued for ten years.

Toward the end of the twenties his company gave him a better job which entailed a lot of travel. He found that a few drinks with agreeable companions, in sleeping cars or hotels, helped pass the time. He frankly preferred the company of those who took a drink or two to those who did not. For the next few years, he had a lot of fun with alcohol and liked its effect.

But soon he began to realize that he needed more alcohol than the others did. In retrospect, he concluded that at this time he was becoming more physically sensitive to and losing his tolerance for alcohol. Soon he began experiencing blackouts and at times would forget where he had parked his car.

Soon traveling, even by train, became a hazard. He would find himself on trains going in the wrong direction and would end up in a town or city where he had no intention of being and had no business to transact.

Time and again he went on the wagon, but sooner or later it would start all over again. Friends and family began speaking to him about his drinking. But the compulsion to drink was growing stronger.

Up to this point his rise in the business world had been steady and he held a fine executive position. But now he was delaying making decisions, putting off appointments, and it was difficult to concentrate or even to follow closely a business conversation. Eventually he was fired. So, he went on the wagon and got another good job. He stayed sober for a year but found that being on the wagon was the most miserable way to exist and fell off again. He could not stop.

Finally, he contacted A.A. His A.A. contact told him: "Today could be the most important day in your life." It was.

He immediately went to the president of the company for whom he then worked and told him he had joined A.A. He got a hearty handshake and an unmistakable look of approval. That was enough. He knew he was on the way up again—as long as he remembered to stay away from the first drink.

He still had his ups and downs, but during his years in A.A. he was continually learning to accept the things he cannot change, being given courage to change the things he could, and the wisdom to know the difference.

A.A. gave him a happy and contented way of living, and he was very deeply grateful to the founders and early members of A.A. who plotted the course and who kept the faith.

New Vision for a Sculptor

Fred (last name unknown), New York City

2nd ed. p. 426

"His conscience hurt him as much as his drinking. But that was years ago."

Fred stopped drinking in May of 1937, after praying to God for help. He was then not quite forty. He joined A.A. in May of 1947.

He had a wonderful childhood. His was a very close family. His parents were very successful, and they had luxury and beauty in their lives and they were truly appreciative of all they had. The family was Jewish, although not orthodox, and keenly alive to the beauty of religion.

His two older brothers were good students, but not artistic. Fred was a very bad student but very much an artist. When he showed talent as a sculptor the entire family encouraged him.

When World War I broke out, he remembered what his parents had told him so often; how grateful he should be to be in the United States. His grandfathers had both come from countries in Europe where Jews were persecuted, and they wanted to live and be a part of the "land of the free."

Because his brothers were both married, he felt he should be the one to join the Army. He was sent to France, where he discovered he could drink everyone else under the table. About three days before the Armistice, he was wounded when a truck he was riding in was blown up. He woke up in Vichy a couple of days later to learn that he had an injury to his spine.

After the war, he seemed to have no problem with alcohol, except when he did drink, he always wanted to out-drink everyone else, and was drinking more and more himself.

He married in 1920, and in 1928 he and his wife visited France with their two children. There he started drinking brandy to help him sleep.

By this time, he had developed a good reputation as an artist and was very successful at his work. When he realized that his family was worried about his drinking, he started drinking at his studio and at bars rather than at home.

This secret drinking caused him to feel very guilty. He was very unhappy and knew his family was unhappy. The worst part was that in his guilt he lost God. He felt he had no right to pray to God, no right to go into the temple or church. When they had lived in Rome, he used to go into one of the cathedrals every night on his way home from work and, to him, a house of God was a house of God and was beautiful and dedicated to His worship. Now he was robbed of God, because he was so ashamed.

One day he was asked to help the crippled son of his "washwoman" Gabrielle, with his artwork. He was happy to do so, but when he arrived he was drunk. At the door he prayed to God to help him. Miraculously he was able to spend two and-a-half hours helping the boy. But when he left he started drinking again. He didn't remember much about the next ten days. But when he remembered how he had prayed to help the crippled boy, he again turned to God for help. He didn't drink again for the next ten years, but said they were miserable years.

A week or two before Decoration Day 1947, a friend asked him how he was doing with his alcohol problem. He answered that he had no alcohol problem and that on Decoration Day he and his wife were going to try a bottle of champagne.

His friend was an A.A. member and asked him, before he took that first drink, to go to a meeting with him. At the meeting the leader stated "Alcoholism is an incurable, progressive disease. Whether you are dry one year, ten years or fifty years, you're still one drink away from a drunk."

Fred's reaction was "Thank God I didn't take that first drink! Thank God I am here."

He remembered what his mother had said years before when he came home drunk. Weeping, she said, "This must be somehow good. This cannot be all negative. Some good must come out of it."

Toward the end of his first A.A. meeting, he heard about the Twelfth Step. Immediately, his mother's words came to his mind. "That's somehow good," he thought. "Thank God," he wrote, "I have been able to turn it into "Somehow good."

Joe's Woes

Joe M., the Bronx, New York

2nd ed. p. 445

"These were only beginning when he hit Bellevue for the thirty-fifth time. He still had the State hospital ahead of him; and even after A.A., a heartbreaking test of his new-found faith."

Joe joined A.A. in April of 1939 but slipped in November 1939 and returned in February 1940.

Joe had been to Bellevue's alcoholic ward thirty-five times. He thought that should qualify him for A.A. because "they don't take you in the Bellevue alcoholic ward for sinus trouble." His first trip to Bellevue was at the age of seventeen, and he was called an alcoholic at eighteen or nineteen. He was in jail perhaps sixty-five or seventy-five times.

He got married in 1926, thinking he would be able to stop drinking, and fathered three children. After eleven years his wife decided to leave with the children, but his sister intervened and suggested that she pay for him to be treated by a psychiatrist. He agreed because he had begun hallucinating. But he did not cooperate with the psychiatrist. The psychiatrist suggested he go back to Bellevue.

They put him in the mental hospital, but he found he could get alcohol there too. His ten-year-old son tried to support the family by shining shoes. A doctor suggested he sign himself out and try to support his family. But he couldn't hold a job and he couldn't stop drinking.

He went from one job to another, until no one would hire him anymore. He would go to his son and tell him his mother had sent him to get the money, and the son never refused him.

Eventually he was arrested for a very serious crime that he didn't remember committing and could have been sent to Sing Sing for fifteen years. But he was sentenced to the State hospital again.

It was there, in early 1939, that a doctor called him into his office to meet Bill W. and five other A.A.s who were trying to get A.A. into the hospital. Some time later he went to his first meeting in South Orange, New Jersey.

For seven months his wife accompanied him to the meetings. The first time he went alone, he didn't stay until the end, but instead got drunk. Three months later he was back in the State Hospital. He knew that A.A. had not failed him. He had failed A.A. He had not been honest with himself or with anybody else. So, he saw a priest at the hospital and took a very thorough fifth step.

For nearly a year he couldn't get a job, so he spent many hours at the A.A. clubhouse on 24th Street.

His wife got pregnant again. It was a very dangerous pregnancy and when she was delivering the baby, he thought she was dying and went to a bar. In the bar he decided to try prayer. He walked out of the bar after having only a ginger ale and went to the clubhouse. About one in the morning, he got a telegram from the hospital. He had a daughter and she was fine. He thanked God that he hadn't had a drink.

It took him seventeen months to get a job. He didn't like the job he got and was going to give it another week and if no other job came along get drunk. Before that week was up, two men he had worked for a long time before showed up at his house and offered him a job. They had heard he was in A.A. and doing all right. He said good news travels fast in A.A.

But tragedy lay ahead. The son who had been shining shoes at the age of ten, on his sixteenth birthday was in a trolley car accident only two blocks from home. He regained consciousness once in the thirteen hours Joe was with him. He seemed to be trying to tell his father "I'm losing this battle, dad, but don't let this throw you."

Joe was going to go on a suicide drunk, and if that didn't work jump out a window. But before he could do that his phone rang. It was an A.A. member in Ohio. He had heard the news and called to tell him not to drink over it. Another called from Connecticut. Others called, and while he was still answering calls an A.A. friend walked in and stayed with him that night. The next morning the undertaker came to take him to the hospital morgue to identify his son. His A.A. friend went with him, and the undertaker was also in A.A.

"Well, when that slab was pulled out for me to identify my son's body, if I didn't have A.A. on my right and A.A. on my left I wouldn't be alive today."

So, his length of sobriety wasn't handed to him on a silver platter. But he was sober over eleven years when he wrote his story, "thanks to the good people of A.A., and last but not least by the Grace of God."

There's Nothing the Matter with Me!

Bill G., New Jersey

2nd ed. p. 499

"That's what the man said as he hocked his shoes for the price of two bottles of Sneaky Pete. He drank bayzo, canned heat, and shoe polish. He did a phony routine in A.A. for a while. And then he got hold of the real thing."

Bill got sober in 1945.

He thought that in his business, the furniture business, you had to drink. You had to drink to celebrate a sale, to drown your sorrows if there isn't a sale.

First he drank only to celebrate or if he was depressed. Then he began drinking all the time. He needed no excuse. This was during Prohibition, so he carried a flask.

Little by little he developed a persecution complex: his business associates said he drank too much, his wife expected him to bring home money on payday; the golf club asked him to resign for not paying his tabs.

He tried a geographic cure. He sold his business, went to Seattle, by way of San Diego, and went into business there and in twenty months was bankrupt. It took him nine months to get back to New Jersey.

Things went from bad to worse and one day he sold his shoes for 75 cents and bought two bottles of Sneaky Pete (cheap muscatel wine with grain alcohol added when it was bottled to further increase its alcohol content) and a pair of "canvas relievers" (presumably cheap canvas slippers) to wear on his feet.

The Salvation Army gave him a bed and put him to work for ninety-five cents a week and his room and board. Soon they were paying him $5 a week. "No drunk can stand prosperity," he wrote, and he got drunk and was out on the street again. But he had a pair of shoes and a gabardine suit much too large for him. He slept under the bridge and drank "bayzo" (Bay Rum aftershave lotion), canned heat, Sneaky Pete, shoe polish, anything that had alcohol in it. He had no sense of responsibility, no moral code, no sense of ethics—nothing.

One day he ran into his wife who took pity on him. She took him to a hospital where the doctor suggested he try A.A. He told his wife A.A. didn't allow women at the meetings, and that they had alcohol there to test them. When he came home smelling of alcohol, he would tell her he had been "testing." When he finally came home dead drunk he said to her "Madam, they put me to the test, and I have failed!"

He called the clubhouse and he and his wife went there. The women took his wife aside and explained A.A. to her, a different version from what he had told her.

At the end of three months they asked him to speak. All he could say was "I'm glad to be here." He sat down to tremendous applause.

Soon he learned that A.A. did not need him, but that he needed A.A. That gave him the beginnings of a little humility. He had divorced himself from the Church when he was twenty-one. But he talked to "Father McNulty" who told him not to worry, "you'll develop an awareness of God."

He did. He began to see God in nature and in people. He would meet someone he knew and the first thing that entered his mind was "What is there good about that guy that I know?" Big people, he said, discuss ideals, average people discuss things, and little people—they just talk about other people. And you realize that if you put this all together, you get a little humility, a little tolerance, a little honesty, a little sincerity, and a little prayer—and a lot of A.A.

Annie the Cop Fighter

Annie C., New York City

2nd ed. p. 514

Annie came to A.A. in April of 1947, at the age of sixty-seven. She was a "scrub lady," poor, and uneducated. She lived in a tenement house on First Avenue.

Her husband had left her, taking the children with him. At one point he invited her to move back with him and she did. She says that by then the oldest boy was married, and the youngest was studying to become a policeman. "Brother!"

She had her first drink at age 31. She fought with police and was frequently arrested for being drunk and disorderly. She cleaned rooms in a hotel but got drunk on an occupant's liquor and fell asleep on his bed. She got fired. At one point she was drinking with the boys on the Bowery.

At her first meeting she met Nancy F. ("The Independent Blonde") who reports "She laughed and said, 'You're jealous of me because I've had a few drinks and you can't have any.'" Nancy replied, "You're so right."

She had a slip, after which she went to High Watch Farm. When she returned Nancy suggested she take the fifth step, either with Dr. Silkworth or with a priest. She chose to do it with a priest. (The priest was probably also an A.A. member.)

She and the priest met at Nancy's apartment. Nancy made coffee and suggested that Annie attend the meeting on 58th Street when they were finished, then left. When Annie arrived at the meeting, she seemed clearly relieved. Even though Nancy had told her this was not a confession, that she was just to tell him her story, she did make a confession. She told the priest: "Father, I'll tell you everything, but don't ask me how many times."

She was a very simple, uninhibited woman. She cursed a lot when she spoke, but then would look at a priest in the audience say, "Excuse me, Father, but I'm trying to be careful."

Nancy was a hairdresser, and when Annie came to the beauty shop, she would charge her a dollar "because I never wanted her to think I just gave her anything because she was very proud." Annie later went to another beauty shop and when they charged her six dollars she said, "Hell, I can get it done for a buck up on Park Avenue."

She is said to have had the time of her life in A.A. She had nothing, but she was sober, and she was having a ball. She was happy as a lark.

Annie died when she was about seventy-four.

The Independent Blonde

Nancy F., New York City

2nd ed. p. 532

Nancy came to A.A. in June 1945, when she was 39 years old. She did not write her own story, which was written by some writers in A.A., and she claims she didn't even know it was in the Big Book.

She left home at fourteen. Her mother had died when she was three, her father remarried when she was fourteen, and her stepmother kicked her out. "When you're thrown out, you don't feel like you're anything. You know something's got to be wrong with you or they wouldn't have thrown you out. And they tell me that, psychologically, I felt abandoned by my mother."

She had made a few geographic "cures," but they didn't work. She kept quitting jobs, not having the courage to wait to be fired.

Her contact with A.A. was at the clubhouse on Ninth Avenue and 41st Street. She expected to meet a bunch of bums, so did not get dressed up because she didn't want to look better than everybody else. When she arrived Park Avenue types were there. "And I was so welcome. It was the first time I felt welcome."

She was impressed on coming to A.A. to meet a countess (Felicia G., "Stars Don't Fall.")

At that time Nancy had a little beauty shop and often gave permanents to members of A.A., both those who could afford to pay her, and those who could not.

She and another young woman, perhaps Marty M., were often asked to go to hospitals and drying-out places frequented by the wealthy, because they were younger and "presentable." They bought little hats with flowers on them and wore little black dresses and pearls on these occasions.

Once they went to the apartment of a celebrated actress, and she told them such wonderful stories, they forgot why they were there.

"We didn't have the nerve to tell her that she was a drunk. Later she did get sober," Nancy said years later.

She didn't like to work with the families in the beginning. "I was mad at the families. I wouldn't talk to anybody but the alcoholic."

"I was so eager to give what I had," she said "I went right from the First Step to the last Step. For me it was just wonderful. I got in with people and I cared for somebody. You see, I had never cared for anybody, not even myself. When you care for somebody, you begin to heal yourself. You don't even know it."

Nancy said everyone in A.A. knew each other in those days because they were all in one clubhouse.

She often went to Dr. Silkworth for advice. "If we were in trouble, we'd go to Dr. Silkworth. If we were in a situation and we didn't know how to get out of it or were afraid we might get drunk, we could talk it over with him. He was a very simple, wonderful man. He said to me once, 'The day that you can sit down and just be honest with yourself in this situation, you will know what to do.' That was the kind of a man he was."

Nancy went to the clubhouse every day from eleven o'clock in the morning when they opened until they closed at night. It was the only place she felt safe.

For the first five years, she did nothing but go to A.A. She didn't know what else to do. For fifteen years she attended a women's meeting that Marty M. started in the home of a woman whose husband was an alcoholic. It was on 58th Street in midtown Manhattan.

Marty wanted to hire her as a speaker for the National Council on Alcoholism, but she declined.

Nancy is a good example of what people can accomplish after they get sober. She went to high school in her fifties and went to college when she was seventy. She went to college for nine and a half years, studied behavioral science, and graduated cum laude.

When she arrived at A.A. she didn't believe in God and didn't want to hear anything about it. But she began searching. Later she became a Quaker and taught English to migrant workers. She was one of the speakers at the 2000 A.A. International Convention in Minneapolis.

Third Edition

PIONEERS OF A.A.

Dr. Bob and the twelve men and women whose stories are in this section were among the early members of A.A.'s first groups. The third edition introduces this section by saying that they all had passed away of natural causes, having maintained complete sobriety. But it is known that Marty M. and Clarence S. were both still living when the third edition was published, and Marty had a later slip of which perhaps the editors of the third edition were unaware.

Dr. Bob's Nightmare

Robert H. S., M.D., Akron, Ohio

Titled THE DOCTOR'S NIGHTMARE
in orig. ms./1st ed.

Orig. ms. and 1st ed. p. 183;
2nd, 3rd and 4th eds. p. 171

"A co-founder of Alcoholics Anonymous. The birth of our Society dates from his first day of permanent sobriety, June 10, 1935. To 1950, the year of his death, he carried the A.A. message to more than 5,000 alcoholic men and women, and to all these he gave his medical services without thought of charge. In this prodigy of service, he was well assisted by Sister Ignatia at St. Thomas Hospital in Akron, Ohio, one of the greatest friends our Fellowship will ever know."

Dr. Bob met Bill Wilson and stopped drinking on Mother's Day, May 12, 1935, but about three weeks later he drank again while on a trip to attend a medical convention. His last drink was June 10, 1935, (or perhaps June 17, 1935, according to some sources).

His son, "Smitty," described him as a very sensitive man, who loved being a doctor, and as "a man's man," who was also very courteous, especially to women. "Women felt comfortable around him, because he so obviously loved my mom." Smitty also describes him as having a great sense of humor.

He was born on August 8, 1879, St. Johnsbury, Vermont, about one hundred miles northeast of East Dorset, where Bill W. was born. He was the only child of Judge and Mrs. Walter P. S., who were influential in business and civic affairs. He had a much older foster sister, Amanda Northrup, of whom he was quite fond.

His parents were pillars of the North Congregational Church in St. Johnsbury. They insisted Bob go to church not only on Sunday, but also several times during the week. He later rebelled against this and decided he wasn't going into a church again except for funerals or weddings. And he didn't—for about forty years. But the religious education stood him in good stead in future years. Smitty said his father was one of the few people he knew who had read the Bible from cover to cover three times.

He entered St. Johnsbury Academy at fifteen. At a dance during his senior year he met Anne Ripley of Oak Park, Illinois, a student at Wellesley on holiday with a friend. It was not a whirlwind marriage. They weren't married until seventeen years later. He first had to finish his education, and later she may have been reluctant to marry him because of his drinking.

Except for a secret taste of hard cider when he was about nine, he didn't drink until he was about nineteen and attending Dartmouth College in New Hampshire, described as "the drinkingest" of the Ivy League schools.

A tattoo he wore the rest of his life was probably from those days at Dartmouth: a dragon and compass tattoo. The dragon wound around his left arm from the shoulder to the wrist. It was blue with red fire. His son thinks "he had to have been drunk to have it put there, and you didn't do something that complicated in a day. When I asked him how he got it, he said, 'Boy, that was a dandy!' And it must have been, too."

He wanted to be a doctor, but for some reason his mother opposed it, so he spent the next three years in Boston, Chicago, and Montreal working. Finally he began studying medicine, first at the University of Michigan, and then at Rush University near Chicago. His drinking interfered with his medical education repeatedly, but he eventually received his medical degree, and secured a coveted internship at City Hospital in Akron. After his two years internship he opened an office.

Soon his alcoholism progressed and he was hospitalized repeatedly. His father sent a doctor to Akron to take him back to Vermont where he stayed for a few months, then he returned to his practice, sufficiently frightened that he did not drink again for some time. During this sober period he married Anne.

During Prohibition he thought it would be safe to try a little drinking, since it would not be possible, so he thought, to get large quantities. But it was easy for doctors to obtain alcohol. He also used sedatives to hide his "jitters." Things went from bad to worse.

In the late 1920s, he decided that he wanted to be a surgeon, perhaps because he would be able to control his schedule more easily in this specialty than he could as a general practitioner. The patients wouldn't be calling him for help all hours of the day or night, so they wouldn't catch him when he was drinking.

He went to Rochester, Minnesota, and studied under the Mayo brothers. He became a rectal surgeon and did nothing but surgery for the balance of his life. But Smitty says that the other doctors knew he was a drunk, so the referrals were scarce and his practice small. (Despite the financial problems, they were able to keep the house during the Great Depression because the Federal Government placed a moratorium on foreclosures.)

When he was introduced to the Oxford Group he tried hard for three years to follow their program, and did a lot of study, both of spirituality and of alcoholism. But it wasn't until Bill Wilson arrived in the spring of 1935 that Dr. Bob found the kind of help he needed—one alcoholic talking to another.

Smitty describes Bill Wilson as being the opposite of his dad and both of them were needed for the success of A.A. He once joked: "If it had been up to my dad, A.A. would never have spread beyond Akron. Had it been up to Bill, they would have sold franchises." On another occasion he said: "Bill was garrulous, Bill was a promoter, Bill was a visionary. I think Bill W. could see further in the world than anyone I've ever known. My dad wasn't that way." (Dr. Bob was quiet, cautious, conservative, steady, insistent on keeping things simple.)

Anne S. died on June 2, 1949. Bill noted that she was "quite literally, the mother of our first group, Akron Number One. In the full sense of the word, she was one of the founders of Alcoholics Anonymous."

Serenely remarking to his attendant, "I think this is it," Dr. Bob died on November 16, 1950. The funeral service was held at the old Episcopal Church by Dr. Walter Tunks, whose answer to a telephone call fifteen years earlier had led to the meeting between Dr. Bob and Bill W. He was buried at Mt. Peace Cemetery, next to Anne.

There is no large monument on his grave. Doctor Bob, who always admonished A.A. to "keep it simple," when he heard that friends were planning a monument, remarked "Annie and I plan to be buried just like other folks." Alcoholics Anonymous itself is Dr. Bob's monument.

The Man on the Bed

Bill D., Akron, Ohio

Titled ALCOHOLICS ANONYMOUS NUMBER THREE in orig. ms./1st ed.

Orig. ms. and 1st ed.;
p. 182 in 2nd, 3rd and 4th eds.

"Pioneer member of Akron's Group No. 1, the first A.A. group in the world. He kept the faith, therefore, he and countless others found a new life."

Bill's date of sobriety was the date he entered Akron's City Hospital for his last detox, June 26, 1935, where Bill Wilson and Dr. Bob visited him on June 28. His wife, Henrietta, recalled years later that she had asked her pastor to try to help him, and had prayed with another that someone who could help would visit him at the hospital. He was a prominent lawyer, had been a city councilman, and was a well-adjusted family man and active in his church. Nonetheless, he had been hospitalized eight times in the past six months because of his alcoholism and got drunk even before he got home. When admitted this time he had DTs and had blacked the eyes of two nurses before they managed to strap him down. A nurse commented that he was a grand chap "when sober."

He walked out of that hospital on July 4, never to drink again. A.A.'s first group dates from that day. Within a week, he was back in court, sober, and arguing a case. The message had been successfully shared a second time. Dr. Bob was no fluke, and apparently you did not have to be indoctrinated by the Oxford Group before the message could take hold.

He immediately began working with Dr. Bob and Bill and went with them to visit Ernie Galbraith ("The Seven Month Slip" in the 1st edition) and others.

Oldtimers in Akron said he was indeed a grand chap, when sober, one of the most engaging people they ever knew. One said: "I thought I was a real big shot because I took Bill Dotson to meetings." Another noted that, though Bill Dotson was influential, he was not an ambitious man in A.A., just a good A.A. If you went to him for help he would help you. He never drove a car, but he went to meetings every night, standing around with his thumbs in his vest like a Kentucky colonel.

A.A.'s first documented court case was one Phil S., who was released to the care of Dr. Bob through the efforts of Bill Dotson, who talked with the judge who agreed to release him.

Bill never submitted his story for the 1st edition. Various theories include (1) he wanted to be paid for the story, (2) he was too prominent a person, (3) he was too humble to have his story appear. But in 1952 he told an interviewer that he hadn't been much interested in the project or perhaps thought it unnecessary. He added that Bill Wilson had come to Akron to record his story, which would appear in the next edition of the book. Perhaps by 1952 he was embarrassed that he'd originally wanted to be paid for the story so didn't mention it. But apparently he cooperated to have it appear in the 2nd edition.

Bill Dotson died September 17, 1954, in Akron. Bill Wilson wrote, "That is, people say he died, but he really didn't. His spirit and works are today alive in the hearts of uncounted A.A.s, and who can doubt that Bill already dwells in one of those many mansions in the great beyond. The force of the great example that Bill set in our pioneering time will last as long as A.A. itself."

He Had to be Shown

Dick S., Akron, Ohio

Titled THE CAR SMASHER in 1st ed., rewritten and renamed for later editions

1st ed. p. 364; p. 193 in 2nd and 3rd eds.

"'Who is convinced against his will is of the same opinion still.' But not this man."

Dick's date of sobriety (according to his story in the 1st edition) was the first week of March 1937. In his revised story, which appears in the 2nd and 3rd editions, he cites February 1937. Perhaps in the 1st edition he was citing the day he left the hospital rather than the date of his last drink.

His brother Paul ("Truth Freed Me" in the 1st edition) preceded him into A.A. and helped twelfth step him.

He was the oldest of three children and his father was an alcoholic. His father died in 1901 when he was eight years old. He quit school and went to work. When he was sixteen his mother remarried and he was given an opportunity to go back to school but he did not do well. He was jealous of his brother, Paul, who did things better than Dick did because he applied himself.

When he was eighteen Dick showed off to a group of friends by ordering a martini, extra dry, not even knowing what it was. He drank nine martinis in less than an hour. This was his first drink and his first drunk. He did not drink again for a year. But blackout drinking had begun at once.

He married at nineteen. He tried to control his drinking, but frequently had blackout drunks. He was in the construction business, but lost money, then went into the crude rubber business. He prospered despite his drinking, but the rubber prosperity fell apart in the twenties.

His marriage deteriorated and they were divorced. He began to think he was insane. He didn't want to neglect his children, but he did; he didn't want to get into fights, but he did; he didn't want to get arrested, but he did; he didn't want to jeopardize the lives of innocent people by driving while intoxicated, but he did.

On one occasion when he was hospitalized after a terrible automobile accident, Sister Ignatia stuck her head in the door and told him she thought they might be able to make something human out of his face after all. He was in the hospital fourteen days but drank again after getting out.

One day after a binge he woke to find his brother, Paul, and Dr. Bob at his bedside. When he asked Dr. Bob if he were ever going to drink again, he answered: "So long as I'm thinking as I'm thinking now, and so long as I'm doing the things I'm doing now, I don't believe I'll ever take another drink."

Dick became a very enthusiastic, hardworking early member. He was one of several unidentified people pictured in the March 1, 1941, *Saturday Evening Post* story, most of whom have their backs to the camera. When a committee was formed to develop plans for the first A.A. International Conference, Dick was elected General Chairman. However, according to Bill W., he was not, at least initially, in favor of a General Service Conference.

Dick stayed close to Dr. Bob until his death. When Dr. Bob traveled to the west coast after his wife Anne's death to renew old acquaintances, Dick accompanied him. He wrote to Bill W. after returning from the trip, reporting on how much good the trip had done Dr. Bob, but complaining about "well-wishing friends—one in particular who stayed four hours and damned near drove him nuts."

Ironically, while Dick's story was titled "The Car Smasher," it was his brother Paul who died as a result of an automobile accident on September 19, 1953. However, both brothers remained completely sober until their respective deaths.

He Thought He Could Drink like a Gentleman

Albert (Abby) G.

2nd and 3rd eds. p. 210

"But he discovered that there are some gentlemen who can't drink."

Abby's date of sobriety was April 1939. Clarence S. was his sponsor. He was one of the Roman Catholics who had some problems about attending Oxford Group meetings.

He was born in Cleveland, Ohio, in 1889, the last child of a family of eight. His parents were hard working people, but his father was a strict disciplinarian. But Abby was slick and cute enough to be safe from his father's discipline. So he grew up thinking rules were for others, not for him. At sixteen he was picked up by the police and brought home drunk. He got expelled from various schools but finally graduated from the eighth grade.

He obtained a job as a toolmaker's apprentice and later worked for large companies and gained experience.

Then he attended a technical high school and at eighteen went to night school to get a high school diploma. He then entered an engineering college, then law school and passed the bar exam. He later became a patent attorney.

He married at twenty-eight, while in law school, and had two children by the time he was admitted to the bar. During this time, he had been too busy to drink much, but about four years after he became a partner in his law firm, he began, like others during Prohibition, making elderberry blossom wine.

Soon there were automobile wrecks, when the police escorted him home, but not to jail. On business trips to New York he would disappear and wind up in Philadelphia or Boston. He began firing clients before they fired him. His partners suffered from his conduct but tolerated it because he still managed to hang onto a very substantial practice.

His wife learned about the fellowship from her hairdresser who told her about her brother-in-law, Clarence S. ("The Home Brewmeister"), who had been quite a drinker, and about some doctor in Akron who had straightened him out. (This was not the same sister-in-law who married Hank P.) For about nine months she prayed constantly that Abby would find this solution that Clarence had found. Her prayers were answered: one day Clarence and his sister-in-law called at the house.

For some reason he didn't like Clarence at first. Clarence thought Abby looked down on him because Abby was an educated man, a patent attorney, and Clarence only had a high school education. But Dorothy S., Clarence's first wife, reported that although Abby was well educated, the person in Akron that made the most impression on him was a man who hadn't gone beyond the fourth grade. (This may have been Dick S., "He Had to be Shown.")

Abby resisted joining A.A., but Clarence would show up at saloons where he was drinking to drag him home. Finally, Bill W., while visiting Cleveland, called on Abby and persuaded him to enter the hospital. Bill and Dorothy S. drove him there. While he was still in the hospital, his wife volunteered their large home as a meeting place in Cleveland. Thus, the first Cleveland meeting was held at Abby's home.

Bill W. gave him credit for starting the principle of rotation of jobs in A.A. Abby had been chairman of the central committee in Cleveland (the first in the nation). It consisted of five men and two women. But Abby was older (in years) than most of the members and had family responsibilities. So he was happy to step down after a few months. He suggested that one man and one woman drop off each month to be replaced by the next in line according to seniority.

Women Suffer Too

Margaret ("Marty") M., New York City and Connecticut

2nd and 3rd eds. p. 222, 4th ed. p. 200

"Despite great opportunities, alcohol nearly ended her life. Early member, she spread the word among women in our pioneer period."

Marty's date of sobriety is uncertain, but she attended her first A.A. meeting at Bill W.'s home in Brooklyn on April 11, 1939 and was an enthusiastic member of A.A. from that day until her death.

She was not the first woman in A.A. The "Lady known as 'Lil'," in Akron, who probably never got sober, and Florence R. ("A Feminine Victory" in the first edition) preceded her.

A recent biography of Marty M. reveals that there was still another woman ahead of her—Mary C.—who visited Marty when she was still at Blythewood Sanitarium in 1939. (This other woman, who was from somewhere in the South, would have been the A.A. woman with the longest sobriety had she not slipped in 1944, although she came back to AA and thereafter stayed sober until her death in the 1990s.)

Marty was one of the first women to enter A.A. and gain long-term sobriety. But she had several slips. Three of these were at the very beginning, between Christmas 1939 and Christmas 1940. The authors of Marty's recent biography found that she then had another slip somewhere between 1959 and 1964, most likely around 1960. She quickly recovered however, and after that stayed continuously sober until her death in 1980.

Marty grew up in Chicago, in a wealthy family. She had every advantage, the best boarding schools and a finishing school in Europe.

A popular debutante, she made her debut in 1927, after which she eloped with John B. of New Orleans. Marty said of him: "He was one of the most attractive men I've met, interesting, traveled, with a keen mind. His family was prominent socially and he was the town's worst drunk." They were both high on alcohol when they eloped. Later a church service was held in New Orleans. Marty, whose alcoholism was not far progressed at the time, could not put up with John's drinking behavior and they were divorced in 1928. She resumed her maiden name and sometime thereafter started to identify herself as "Mrs. Marty M." She never remarried.

Her divorce coincided with her father's bankruptcy and Marty went to work. For the next ten years she did whatever she wanted to do. For greater freedom and excitement she went abroad to live. She ran a successful business. Headstrong and willful, she rushed from pleasure to pleasure. But her alcoholism got out of hand and soon she was in real trouble and attempted suicide twice. She came home to America, broke and desperate. Things got even worse.

She entered Bellevue Hospital's neurology ward under the care of Robert Foster Kennedy, M.D. Eventually she entered Blythewood Sanitarium, as a charity patient, under the care of Dr. Harry Tiebout, who gave her the manuscript of the Big Book to read and arranged for her to go to her first meeting.

She said "I went trembling into a house in Brooklyn filled with strangers and I found I had come home at last, to my own kind. There is another meaning for the Hebrew word that in the King James version of the Bible is translated 'salvation.' It is: 'to come home.' I had found my salvation. I wasn't alone anymore."

In a July 1968 Grapevine update of her story, Marty said the Twelve Steps were still very important to her. They gave her more than sobriety. They gave her a glimpse at something she had never known peace of mind, a sense of being comfortable with herself and with the world in which she lived, and a lot of other things which could be summed up as a sense of growth, both emotional and spiritual.

Marty was a visionary and a pioneer who took on an unpopular cause during an era when women were supposed to remain silent. With the encouragement of Bill W., Marty founded the National Council on Alcoholism, through which she educated the general public about alcoholism and helped shape the modern alcoholism movement.

She wrote two authoritative books on alcoholism: *Marty Mann's Primer on Alcoholism* in 1950 (which was rewritten and published as *Marty Mann's New Primer on Alcoholism* in 1958), and *Marty Mann Answers Your Questions About Drinking and Alcoholism* in 1970.

Marty influenced alcoholism legislation at the State and national levels. She is considered to be "the mother of the Hughes Act," the Comprehensive Alcohol Abuse and Alcoholism Prevention, Treatment, and Rehabilitation Act of 1970, which greatly enhanced the federal government's role in alcoholism treatment and prevention.

Mel B., in *My Search for Bill W.*, described Marty as one of Bill W.'s closest friends and allies. "A refined, attractive woman, she impressed me as being the kind of person who can handle great responsibilities with confidence and ease. While some men may have felt threatened by such a strong woman, Bill supported her work and went out of his way to encourage her."

To protect the work she was doing during a period of heavy anti-gay bias, Marty never revealed her lesbianism except to Bill (her sponsor) and other close friends. Her long-time lesbian partner was Priscilla P., once a glamorous art director at *Vogue* magazine, the fifth woman Marty brought into A.A. In her last years Marty was deeply troubled by Priscilla's Alzheimer's disease.

Marty made her last public appearance at the A.A. International Convention in New Orleans in July of 1980. She arrived in a wheelchair, but after she was introduced she rose and walked to the podium to thunderous applause and a prolonged ovation.

Two weeks after her return to her home in Easton, Connecticut, her housekeeper found her unconscious at the kitchen table. She had suffered a massive cerebral hemorrhage the night before. Priscilla had slept through it all. She was rushed to St. Vincent's Medical Center in Bridgeport, CN, where she died later that night, July 22, 1980, at the age of 75.

The New York Times ran a major obituary, and her death was widely reported around the nation. A long tribute to her was read into the Congressional Record.

When Priscilla died on November 9, 1982, Marty's brother tried to make arrangements for her to be buried next to Marty in Chicago, but Rosehill Cemetery ruled that the family plot was reserved for members of the family only. Priscilla was cremated and her remains spread on the waters off the coast on the shore of Connecticut.

The European Drinker

Joe D., Cleveland, Ohio

Orig. ms., 1st ed. p. 206, 2nd and 3rd eds. p. 230

"Beer and wine were not the answer."

Joe's date of sobriety was April 1936. He was twelfth stepped by Dr. Bob, and was probably the first Roman Catholic in A.A.

He was born in Germany and grew up on "good Rhine wine of song and story." His parents wanted him to become a priest and he attended a Franciscan school at Basle, Switzerland. But although he was a good Catholic, the monastic life did not appeal to him, so he became a harness-maker and upholsterer.

He drank about a quart of wine a day, which was common in his part of the world. Everybody drank wine.

He did his compulsory military service and took part in the Boxer Rebellion in China. There he experimented with more potent beverages. When he returned to Germany he resumed his wine drinking.

At age twenty-four, he came to America and settled in Cleveland where he had relatives. He founded a mattress factory and was doing well with his general upholstering work, and there was every indication that he would be financially independent by the time he was middle aged. By this time he was married and was paying for a home.

He thought American wine inferior to German so drank beer instead. When Prohibition became law he quit drinking altogether, since he couldn't get what he liked. He hardly tasted anything for two years.

Soon, like his friends, he began to drink home-brew, which was a lot stronger than he had been used to. More and more he started doing some of his business in the speakeasy. There he could buy whiskey, which was easier to transport than beer or wine, and he developed a taste for hard liquor.

It soon became obvious that he had a problem with alcohol. He became a periodic drinker and was eased out of the business he had founded and was reduced to doing general upholstery in a small shop at the back of his house.

His wife complained about his drinking, so he hid bottles all over the house. At times he would resolve never to drink again and pour out full pints and smash the bottles, only to find himself frantically searching for any he missed so he could have a drink.

He began to absence himself from the church where he had formerly been a member of the choir. He never asked the priest to give him the pledge like many other Catholic alcoholics did. (It was common at that time for Roman Catholics who had problems with alcohol to pledge to a priest that they would stop drinking. It usually didn't work if the man was an alcoholic.)

Then occurred the event that saved him. Dr. Bob visited him. He did not ask any questions except whether he was definite about his desire to quit drinking. There were no more than four or five in Dr. Bob's group at the time, but they befriended him. He was advised "You've been trying man's ways and they always fail. You can't win unless you try God's way."

He had no problem with what they were teaching him because his church taught the same thing. He put into practice what he was being taught and soon Dr. Bob sent him to talk to other alcoholics.

The first few months were hard: business trials, little worries, and feelings of general despondency nearly drove him to the bottle, but he made progress in the spiritual life.

"As I go along, I seem to get strength daily to be able to resist more easily. And when I get upset, cross-grained and out of tune with my fellow man I know that I am out of tune with God. Searching where I have been at fault, it is not hard to discover and get right again, for I have proven to myself and to many others who know me that God can keep a man sober if he will let him."

Dorothy S., the wife of Clarence S. ("The Home Brewmeister"), was eager to help this group reach other alcoholics. She approached Rev. Dilworth Lupton, of the First Unitarian Church in Cleveland, concerning the group, but he was negative about the Oxford Group and wanted nothing to do with it. After the Cleveland members broke away from the Oxford Group, she approached him again, this time with a copy of the book and with the names of some Roman Catholics who were members. Among the names was that of Joe D. The fact Joe D. was associated with this new Cleveland group was sufficient proof to Reverend Lupton that the alcoholic fellowship had indeed broken with the Oxford Group, and he offered to help in any way he could.

He preached a sermon called "Mr. X. and Alcoholics Anonymous," which Dorothy arranged to have covered by the press. It was later made into one of the first pamphlets used by Cleveland A.A.

The Vicious Cycle

Jim B., Washington, D.C.

2nd and 3rd eds. p. 238, 4th ed. p. 219

"How it finally broke a Southerner's obstinacy and destined this salesman to start A.A. at Philadelphia."

Jim was twelfth stepped into the fellowship on January 8, 1938. But he had a slip in June of that year. His last drink was June 16, 1938.

He was described as having red hair, and being rather slim, at least in his last years.

He spent his early life in Baltimore where his father was a physician and a grain merchant. They lived in very prosperous circumstances, and while both parents drank, sometimes too much, they were not alcoholics. Home life was reasonably harmonious. There were four children, and both of his brothers later became alcoholics. One of his brothers died from alcoholism. His sister never took a drink in her life.

He attended public schools until thirteen, then was sent to an Episcopal school for boys in Virginia where he stayed four years. But there he developed a real aversion to all churches and established religions. At school they had Bible readings before each meal and church services four times on Sunday.

At seventeen he entered the university to please his father who wanted him to study medicine as he had. There he took his first drink and he always remembered it. He blacked out the first time he drank.

In the spring of 1917, because he feared he would be kicked out of school, he joined the Army. Due to his OTC training, he entered with the rank of sergeant, only later to come out a private.

During his military service he became a periodic alcoholic. On November 5, 1918, the troops heard a false report that the Armistice would be signed the next day, so Jim had a couple of cognacs to celebrate, then hopped a truck and went AWOL. His next thing he knew he was in Bar le Duc, many miles from base. It was November 11. The bells were ringing and whistles blowing for the real Armistice.

Back in the States he migrated from job to job, unable to hold any for very long. The boss who fired him from one job was Hank P. ("The Unbeliever" in the 1st edition). In the eight years before he stopped drinking, he had over forty jobs.

Finally, January 8, 1938, his boyhood friend Fitz M. ("Our Southern Friend") sent one of his early sponsees, Jackie W., to try to help him. When Jackie got drunk Jim called New York and was told that the two of them should come to New York. Hank, who had fired him eleven years before, offered Jim a job working with him and Bill W. at Honor Dealers. (See bottom of page 149 of the Big Book.) Hank fired him again, at least briefly, when he had his slip in June of that year.

Jim met his wife, Rosa, on a twelfth step call (the only time he ever twelfth stepped a woman). They were married a year later, and reportedly both did much service work in A.A. and were elected to various offices.

On February 13, 1940, with about two years of sobriety, Jim moved to the Philadelphia area and started a group there. He also helped start A.A. in Baltimore.

He wrote a history of A.A. in Philadelphia, and also wrote a history called "The Evolution of Alcoholics Anonymous." It contains some factual errors and his memory differed in spots from some of the other early A.A. members and of Bill W., but it is the first historical piece written about A.A.

Jim is usually given credit for the third tradition, that the only requirement for membership is a desire to stop drinking. He also is credited with the use of "God as we understood Him" in the Steps. (Jim, an agnostic, was militantly opposed to too much talk of God in the Big Book, but he said later that his agnostic stance had mellowed over the years.)

When he updated his story for the May 1968 edition of the A.A. *Grapevine*, he told how in the early days in New York he started fighting all the things Bill and the others stood for, especially religion, the "God bit." But he did want to stay sober and did love the understanding Fellowship. Soon he was number four in seniority in the New York group.

He said he learned later that the New York group had a prayer meeting on what to do with him. The consensus seemed to have been that they hoped he would either leave town or get drunk. He added that his spiritual growth over the past thirty years had been very gradual and steady.

Later he moved to San Diego, California, where he lived until his death. After breaking his hip in a freak accident from which he never fully recovered, Jim was often in a wheelchair. Following a long illness, he was admitted to the Veterans Administration Medical Center, La Jolla, California, where he started an A.A. meeting which still meets on Thursday nights.

Jim died in the VA hospital on September 8, 1974. He and Fitz M. are buried just a few yards apart on the grounds of Christ Episcopal Church at Owensville, Maryland.

The News Hawk

Jim S., Akron, Ohio

Titled TRAVELER, EDITOR, SCHOLAR in 1st ed.

Orig. ms., 1st ed. p. 254, 2nd and 3rd eds. p. 251

"This newsman covered life from top to bottom, but he ended up, safely enough, in the middle."

Jim's date of sobriety was July 1937. He was described as tall and skinny, and a real lone wolf.

He was born in Australia, and it is uncertain when he first came to America. He received a liberal arts education and apparently married while in college or soon after.

Jim had itchy feet and soon after college, estranged from his family, he went to Great Britain where he became a bookmaker's clerk on the British racing circuits, and was far better off financially than the average professional man. When money was missing, he was fired and he sailed for New York, knowing he was through among the English "bookies."

He continued to travel far and wide, working at a variety of jobs in many cities in this country and abroad, and he also spent some periods as a hobo. On one occasion he left his wife and baby in Scotland and sailed for New York.

Many of his jobs were with newspapers, the first one in Pittsburgh. While working on a newspaper in Ohio he stayed sober for two years, except for a one-night drunk in Chicago, and kept a quart of medicinal whiskey in his apartment to taper off the occasional newspaper alcoholics who were sent to see him. He stayed sober for a total of four years, the last two during World War I when he served in a Canadian regiment.

Discharged in 1919 he made up for his dry spell: Quebec, Toronto, Buffalo, and Pittsburgh, were the scenes of man-sized drunks until he had gone through his readjustment discharge pay. He again became a reporter on a Pittsburgh paper.

He was working in a large Ohio city when his wife came over from Scotland to join him. The new job lasted five years. He quit that job and moved to Washington, D.C., then Texas.

Washed up in Texas he returned to the town he had left five years before. His wife made several attempts to get him to stop drinking, but without success.

While working in a small bookstore Jim was called to a hospital to see a friend with whom he had once worked. (This man was probably Earl T., "He Sold Himself Short.") His friend had insisted he visit. He was hospitalized for alcoholism and was already reaching out to help Jim. A few days later another man came into his shop to talk to him about a plan for recovery and invited him to a meeting. But Jim insisted he was on the wagon and doing fine.

It wasn't long before he was on another bender, which lasted until his friend from the hospital picked Jim up and put him in the hospital.

In the interim he may have lost his job at the bookstore, since one report says that Dr. Bob found Jim on skid row selling hair oil and panhandling. But according to Jim's story, he didn't meet Dr. Bob until he was in the hospital.

After Jim's recovery began, knowing he had been a journalist, Dr. Bob, asked him if he would help the Akron and Cleveland members write their stories. He took on the job gladly, urging them to get their stories on paper, and nagging them when they dragged their feet. He edited and rewrote some of the stories but tried to keep the flavor of the original version.

From Farm to City

Ethel M., Akron, Ohio

2nd and 3rd eds. p. 261

"She tells how A.A. works when the going is rough. A pioneer woman member of A.A.'s first Group."

Ethel's date of sobriety was May 8, 1941. She was the first woman to get sober in Akron.

She came from a very poor family, the oldest in a family of seven. Her father was an alcoholic. They moved from the country to the city when she was at an age where girls want nice things and to be like the other girls at school. She felt the others were making fun of her and feared that she wasn't dressed as well as the rest.

At the age of sixteen she was invited to spend the summer with an aunt in Liberty, Indiana. Her aunt told her she could have boyfriends visit, but that she must stay away from one boy, Russ M. (his name was Roscoe, but he was called Rollo or Russ), who came from a fine family but drank too much. Four months later, she married him, even though he drank and he was seven years her senior. She was sure his family disapproved of her because she was from the wrong side of the tracks.

They had two daughters, but about seven or eight years after they were married his drinking became so bad that she took her children and went home. She didn't see Russ or hear from him for a year. She was about twenty-five at the time and had never touched a drop of alcohol.

At the end of a year the children received a card from their father, which she kept and cherished. It said, "Tell Mommy I still love her." Soon Russ himself arrived. She welcomed him with open arms, though he had little but the clothes on his back. He told her he would never drink again and she believed him.

He got a job and went back to work and stayed "dry" for thirteen years. By the end of the thirteen years their older daughter was married and she and her husband were living with them, and the other daughter was in her last year of high school.

Then one night their son-in-law and Russ went to a prizefight. Russ came home drunk. She told him, "The children are raised, and if this is the way you want it, this is the way we'll have it. Where you go I'll go, and what you drink I'll drink." And thus Ethel started drinking.

They went on vacations in the car, drinking all the way. Ethel did the driving. One Sunday afternoon she got picked up for drunk driving and they both were thrown in jail. On another occasion she got drunk and set the house on fire.

In 1940 they read something about A.A. in the newspaper. They talked about it and thought there might come a time when they needed it.

She was having a drink in a barroom one day and told the woman behind the bar she wished she never had to take another drink. She was told to talk to Jack, the owner of the place, whom they had always tried to buy a drink, but who always refused saying he couldn't handle alcohol. (This may have been John M., one of the early Cleveland members.)

Finally, one morning Ethel got in the car and cried all the way to that bar and told them she was licked and wanted help. But Jack was out and his wife said she would send him as soon as he returned. He soon arrived with two cans of beer: one for Ethel and one for Russ. That was their last drink. Men from A.A. started coming to the house the next day, telling their stories, and Jack brought them the *Saturday Evening Post* story about A.A., and told them the whole thing was based on the Sermon on the Mount. Paul S. visited and stressed that they read the Big Book.

So many nicely dressed people were coming in nice cars that Ethel told Russ: "I suppose the neighbors say, 'Now those old fools must have up and died, but where's the hearse?'"

Jack took them to a meeting at the King School on Wednesday night and introduced Ethel to some of the wives. Annabelle G., the wife of Wally G. ("Fired Again" in the 1st edition), was told to take her under her wing. Ethel never forgot how she "sort of curled up her nose and said, 'They tell me you drink too.'" Ethel often thought how that would turn some people away, but she replied: "Why sure, that's what I'm here for."

Women had a harder time being accepted in Akron than they did in New York. Perhaps the reason Ethel was accepted is that Russ joined at the same time. Also Ethel weighed 300 pounds, and the wives probably did not consider her a threat. (Her husband was about half her weight and only about 5'2".)

Ethel gave a lot of credit to Dr. Bob and Anne for their recovery. Dr. Bob and Anne S. spent at least an evening a week at Russ and Ethel M.'s home, and Russ thought Dr. Bob thoroughly enjoyed these visits.

She and Russ worked as a team and were very active from the beginning. Ethel started what may have been the first women's A.A. group.

Her husband died on September 4, 1944. After his death, A.A. became Ethel's whole life and she sponsored many women. She died on April 9, 1963.

The Man Who Mastered Fear

Archie T., Grosse Point, Michigan

Titled THE FEARFUL ONE in 1st ed.,
rewritten and renamed for the later editions

Orig. ms.; 1st ed. p. 332; 2nd and
3rd eds. p. 275; 4th ed. p. 246

"He spent eighteen years in running away; and then found he didn't have to run. So he started A.A. in Detroit."

Archie's date of sobriety was November 1938.

He came from a good upper middle class family in Grosse Point, Michigan. By the time he was twenty-one he had lived in foreign countries for six years, spoke three languages fluently, and had attended college for two years.

Then, family financial difficulties necessitated his going to work. He entered the business world with every confidence that success lay ahead. He had endless dates and went to countless dances, balls and dinner parties.

But this was suddenly shattered when he had a devastating nervous breakdown. Doctors could find nothing physically wrong with him. Psychiatry might have helped, but psychiatrists were little known in his town at that time.

Recovery from the nervous breakdown came very slowly. He ventured out of the house for a walk but became frightened by the time he reached the corner. Gradually he was able to do more, and even to work at various jobs. He found that alcohol helped relieve his many fears.

His parents both died when he was thirty, leaving him a sheltered and somewhat immature man, on his own. He moved into a "bachelor hall," where the men all drank on Saturday nights and enjoyed themselves. Archie drank with them, but also drank himself to sleep every night.

With bravery born of desperation and abetted by alcohol, he married a young and lovely girl. But the marriage lasted only four years, then she took their baby boy and left. He locked himself in the house and stayed drunk for a month.

The next two years he had less and less work and more and more whisky. He ended up homeless, jobless, penniless and rudderless, the problem guest of a close friend whose family was out of town. When the family returned his friend turned Archie over to a couple, perhaps Oxford Group members, who knew Dr. Bob, and who were willing to drive him to Akron. The only stipulation they made was that he had to make the decision himself. What choice did he have? Suicide or finding out whether this group of strangers could help him.

Dr. Bob put him in the hospital for a few days. He then stayed with Dr. Bob and Anne for ten months. He was in bad shape physically, mentally, and spiritually. At first Dr. Bob thought he was "kind of simple."

He was penniless, jobless, and too ill to get out during the day to look for work. Anne nursed him back to health, and while in their home he got down on his knees one day for the first time in thirty years. "God. For eighteen years I have been unable to handle this problem. Please let me turn it over to you." Immediately, a great feeling of peace descended on him, intermingled with a feeling of being suffused with a quiet strength.

He did not want to go back to Michigan, preferring to go someplace where he could make a fresh start. But Detroit was where he had to return, not only because he must face the mess he had made there, but also because it was where he could be of the most service to A.A. In the spring of 1939, Bill W. stopped off in Akron on his way to Detroit on business. He invited Archie to accompany him to Detroit. They spent two days there together before Bill returned to New York.

He made amends where he could and delivered dry cleaning out of a broken-down jalopy to his one-time fashionable friends in Grosse Point. With a nonalcoholic friend, Sarah Klein, he started an A.A. group in Detroit.

He Sold Himself Short

Earl T., Chicago, Illinois

2nd and 3rd eds. p. 287, 4th ed. p. 258

"But he found that there was a Higher Power which had more faith in him than he had in himself. Thus, A.A. was born in Chicago."

Earl's date of sobriety was originally April 1937. He had a brief slip in July of 1937.

He grew up in a small town near Akron, Ohio. Due to his interest in athletics and his parents' influence, he didn't drink or smoke till after high school. All this changed when he went to college, but still he confined his drinking to weekends, and he seemed to drink normally in college and for several years thereafter.

After he left school he lived with his parents and worked in Akron. When he drank he hid it from his parents. This continued until he was twenty-seven. He then started traveling on his job throughout the United States and Canada. This gave him freedom and with an unlimited expense account he was soon drinking every night, not only with customers, but alone.

In 1930 he moved to Chicago. With the Depression limiting his opportunity for employment, and with a lot of time on his hands, he began drinking in the morning. By 1932 he was going on two or three-day benders.

His wife became fed up and called his father to take him back to Akron. For the next five years he bounced back and forth between Chicago and Akron to sober up.

In January of 1937, back in Akron with his father to be sobered up, his father told him about the group in Akron who had the same problem but had found a way to stay sober. Earl knew two of them, one of them Howard, an ex-doctor, whom he had once seen mooching a dime for a drink. He didn't think he was that bad and would have none of it. He told his father he could lick it on his own. He said he would drink nothing for a month and after that only beer.

Several months later his father was back in Chicago to pick him up again, but this time his attitude had changed, and he was willing to talk to the men in Akron. When they got to Akron they routed Howard out of bed. He spent two hours talking to Earl that night.

He was indoctrinated by eight or nine men, after which he was allowed to attend his first meeting, which was led by Bill D. ("A.A. Number Three"). There were eight or nine alcoholics at the meeting and seven or eight wives. There was no Big Book yet and no literature except various religious pamphlets. The meeting lasted an hour and closed with the Lord's Prayer. Then they had coffee and doughnuts and more discussion until the small hours of the morning.

He stayed in Akron two or three weeks and spent a lot of time with Dr. Bob, who took him through the steps in one afternoon. Dr. Bob helped with the moral inventory by pointing out some of his bad personality traits or character defects. Earl wished every alcoholic could have the benefit of this type of sponsorship today.

He returned to Chicago in 1937 to start A.A. there. He got angry and got drunk when his wife criticized his coffee drinking and smoking. (Earl is the heavy smoker and coffee drinker mentioned at the end of the chapter on "The Family Afterward" in the Big Book.) When he slipped, he realized that the alcoholic has to continue to take his own inventory every day if he expects to get well and stay well.

Soon Dan Craske, M.D., began referring prospects to him, and another doctor in Evanston referred a woman named Sylvia K. ("The Keys to the Kingdom"). Earl suggested she go to Akron. There they dried her out and explained the program to her, after which it was suggested that she return to Chicago to work with Earl.

It was Earl who urged Bill W. to codify the A.A. experience, resulting in Bill writing "Twelve Points to Assure Our Future," first published in the April 1946 A.A. *Grapevine*. These are now known as the long form of the traditions. Earl later urged him to shorten them to the Twelve Traditions as we know them today.

Home Brewmeister

Clarence S., Cleveland, Ohio

Orig. ms., 1st ed. p. 274, 2nd and 3rd eds. p. 297

"An originator of Cleveland's Group No. 3, this one fought Prohibition in vain."

Clarence had his last drink on February 11, 1938, according to the article he wrote for the A.A. *Grapevine* November 1968 issue. Fifteen months later he organized the first Cleveland group.

Clarence was born on December 26, 1902, in Cleveland, Ohio, the youngest of three brothers. He dropped out of high school at fourteen, after his father's death, and went to work. He later took many night courses studying economics, business, credits, and collections. This prepared him for later employment at the City National Bank in Cleveland, from which he was fired for alcoholism at the age of thirty-two. It was not the only job from which he was fired.

After holding good positions, making better than average income for over ten years, he was bankrupt in every way. He was in debt, he had no clothes to speak of, no money, no friends, and no one any longer tolerated him except his wife, not even his son or the saloonkeepers. He was unemployable. He said in a talk he gave in 1965 that he couldn't even get a job with the WPA. His wife Dorothy, who worked for an employment agency, couldn't even get him a job.

Then Dorothy heard of a doctor in Akron who had been successful in treating alcoholics. She offered him the alternative of going to see Dr. Bob or her leaving for good. He agreed and that was the turning point in his life. He entered the hospital (after first going on a three-day drunk). While in the hospital a plan for living was explained to him, a simple plan that he found great joy and happiness in following.

He became an enthusiastic twelfth stepper, literally dragging prospects for A.A. off bar stools.

Clarence started the first A.A. group in Cleveland in 1939, in part because some Roman Catholic priests in Cleveland were refusing to let Catholics from their city attend the Oxford Group meeting in Akron.

This was the first group to use the name Alcoholics Anonymous. Nell Wing, Bill W.'s long-time secretary, said that Bill had been using the name since 1938 in letters and a pamphlet, but on this slender basis, Clarence forever claimed to have founded A.A.

Dorothy also was very active and did much to help A.A. in Cleveland. They were divorced before Clarence was drafted into the Army in 1942. Dorothy and their son moved to California.

Unfortunately, Clarence had an abrasive personality, and as one of his friends said, you either loved him or hated him. According to Nell Wing, had he not been so abrasive he probably would have been considered a co-founder of A.A.

When Clarence left Cleveland for military service a farewell party was held for him and he was presented with a wristwatch as a gift from all the West Side groups who acclaimed him for his pioneer work in Cleveland and particularly on the West Side. In a letter from basic training, Private Clarence S. said the going was rough, and he wished he were fifteen or twenty years younger. He supplied his address at Fort Knox, Kentucky, for anyone who wished to write him, and said he missed the association of the groups and was looking for other A.A. members in Kentucky.

He became very hostile toward Bill W. He opposed the traditions and continued to use his full name in public. He led a small group to oppose the Conference and the General Service Office.

After the war he married his second wife, Selma, who worked at the Deaconess Hospital, where her father was the director. Clarence often took alcoholics there to sober them up. Clarence and Selma moved to St. Petersburg, Florida. Eventually they divorced.

Clarence then married his third wife, Grace (also an A.A. member), and joined her as a member of the Assembly of God Church in Winter Park. They did much A.A. work together and conducted many religious retreats. Unlike Bill W., he always used his full name in public, and was honored with several prestigious awards for public service during his life, which he did not hesitate to accept.

He remained very active in A.A., and his A.A. work became increasingly Christian fundamentalist in nature. He and Grace lived at 142 S. Lake Triplet Drive in Casselberry, Florida, until his death on March 22, 1984.

He was buried in Cameron Cemetery in Cameron, North Carolina, in Grace's family plot.

The Keys of the Kingdom

Sylvia K., Chicago, Illinois

2nd and 3rd eds. p. 304, 4th ed. p. 268

"This worldly lady helped to develop A.A. in Chicago and thus passed her keys to many."

According to member list index cards kept by the Chicago group, Sylvia's date of sobriety was September 13, 1939. Because of slips by Marty M. ("Women Suffer Too") Sylvia may have been the first woman to achieve long term sobriety.

Sylvia was raised in a good environment with loving and conscientious parents and given every advantage: the best schools, summer camps, resort vacations and travel. She had her first drink at sixteen and loved what it did for her.

She was the product of the post-war prohibition era of the roaring '20s. She married at twenty, had two children, and was divorced at twenty-three. This gave her a good excuse to drink. By twenty-five she had developed into an alcoholic.

She began making the rounds of the doctors in the hope that one of them might find a cure for her accumulating ailments, most of whom prescribed sedatives and advised rest and moderation.

Between the ages of twenty-five and thirty she tried everything. She moved to Chicago thinking a new environment would help. She tried all sorts of things to control her drinking: the beer diet, the wine diet, timing, measuring, and spacing of drinks. Nothing worked.

The next three years saw her in sanitariums, once in a ten-day coma from which she very nearly died. She wanted to die but had lost the courage to try.

For about one year prior to this time there was one doctor who did not give up on her. He tried everything he could think of, including having her go to mass every morning at six a.m., and performing the most menial labor for his charity patients. This doctor apparently had the intuitive knowledge that spirituality and helping others might be the answer.

In 1939 this doctor heard of the book *Alcoholics Anonymous* and wrote to New York for a copy. After reading it he tucked it under his arm and called on Sylvia. That visit marked the turning point of her life.

He must have studied the book carefully because he took its advice. He gave her the cold, hard facts about her condition, and that she would either die of acute alcoholism, develop a wet brain, or have to be put away permanently.

Then he told her of the handful of people in Akron and New York who seemed to have worked out a technique for arresting their alcoholism. He asked her to read the book and to talk with a man who was experiencing success by using this plan. This was Earl T. ("He Sold Himself Short"), whom she refers to as "Mr. T." in her story.

Earl suggested she visit Akron. According to Bill W., she got off to a slow start there, and may also have been a pill addict. She took a lot of "little white pills" which she claimed were saccharin, and no one could understand why she was so rubber legged. A nurse was flown in, presumably from Chicago, to take care of her.

Sylvia stayed two weeks at the home of Clarence S. ("The Home Brewmeister") and Dorothy S. in Cleveland. She met Dr. Bob, who brought other A.A. men to meet her. Dorothy S. said that the men "were only too willing to talk to her after they saw her." Sylvia was a glamorous divorcee, extremely good looking, and rich. But these attractions probably did not help her with the wives of the alcoholics, who were known on occasion to run women out.

After meeting Dr. Bob she wanted to move to Akron, but this caused great consternation, since her presence threatened to disrupt the whole group. Someone told her it would mean a great deal more if she could go back and help in Chicago.

She went back to Chicago where she eventually got sober. She worked closely with Earl T., and her personal secretary, Grace C., became the first secretary at the Intergroup office in Chicago, the first in the country.

Sylvia updated her story in the January 1969 issue of the A.A. *Grapevine*. She tells how busy her first ten years in A.A. were, but how all this tremendous activity, by bringing her into almost constant contact with other members, provided her with everything she most desperately needed to save her life. As she looked back, she realized this was the most excitingly beautiful period of her life.

When she wrote this update, Sylvia had been living in Sarasota, Florida, with her husband, Dr. Ed S. They were soon to celebrate their eighteenth wedding anniversary. "He is an alky, too, and our lives have been enriched by our mutual faith and perseverance in the A.A. way of life. Through it we have found a quality of happiness and serenity that, we believe, could not have been realized in any other way. Small wonder our gratitude knows no bounds."

THEY STOPPED IN TIME

Too Young?

Author unknown

3rd ed. p. 317

"Sergeants, doctors, girl friends—everybody seemed to be picking on him. But he couldn't be an alcoholic at his age, could he?"

This man was only twenty-four years old when he wrote his story for the 3rd edition. He started drinking about age thirteen.

He didn't do well in school so quit at seventeen and joined the Army. He was in trouble from the beginning. While still in basic training he got drunk almost every night. He couldn't take orders from the head cook when on K.P. and threw a garbage can at him. He was reported to the company commander. After basic training he didn't drink for three months because he was in school at night. He thought this meant he had no drinking problem.

He was sent to Viet Nam where he stayed drunk or sick from a hangover for a year. When he came back from Nam he met a girl he liked, but she would not put up with his drinking and told him to leave.

Next he was sent to Arizona where his drinking increased even more and he started having blackouts and was thrown in jail for speeding and drunk driving. Then he re-enlisted and was sent back to Viet Nam. There he tried suicide twice and wanted to kill his sergeant, so they sent him to a psychiatrist.

When he returned to the States he met a wonderful girl and got engaged. But she soon dropped him, and he still couldn't believe it was his drinking.

He began needing a drink in the morning, and missing work because he was still too drunk to stand up. He became very paranoid and thought everyone was against him. It was the same when they sent him to Germany.

He began hallucinating, and was finally hospitalized, but drank again as soon as he was released. He finally realized he couldn't quit. He talked to the first sergeant and the battalion commander and they put him in contact with an A.A. member.

He had trouble trusting the A.A. members and admitting he was an alcoholic, but eventually did. But he still couldn't stop drinking so was hospitalized again, this time in a rehabilitation center. When he got out he continued to go to A.A. and finally realized that the people in the groups only wanted to help him get sober and to stay sober themselves.

A.A.'s Twelve Steps showed him the way to sobriety, if he wanted it. And he wanted it. A.A. gave him a new way of life. He did have a slip, but was told not to worry about yesterday, because nobody can change it, and not to worry about tomorrow, because it hasn't come yet. Live twenty-four hours at a time. And it works. He said "I'm a twenty-four-year-old alcoholic—and I'm happy."

Fear of Fear

Ceil F. (Ceil M.?), New York City

2nd ed. p. 330; 3rd ed. p. 321; 4th ed. p. 289

"This lady was cautious. She decided she wouldn't let herself go in her drinking. And she would never, never take that morning drink!"

Ceil's date of sobriety was, according to one source, July 1949. Her husband George joined shortly before she did.

She thought she was not an alcoholic, that her problem was that she had been married to a drunk. But she finally admitted, to a woman she met when she accompanied George to the Greenwich Village Group, that she, too, had a problem.

She was one who never went to a hospital, never lost a job, and had never been to jail. And she didn't drink in the morning. Nonetheless, she was a severe alcoholic. She believes that she should have lost her husband, but the fact that he was an alcoholic too kept them together.

She wrote an update of her story for the September 1968 A.A. *Grapevine*. In it she tells how dramatically their lives had changed. When they came to A.A. they were spiritually, mentally, and physically beaten people. Their children were ashamed of them, their families did not want any part of them.

She reported that now their families trusted them again, and physically they were in better shape than they were when they came in. Their friends were all in the fellowship.

George had found it tough going financially for a while, so the women in A.A. suggested she get a job.

She went to work for a New York advertising agency as a receptionist, but soon gained the confidence to look for a better job with more responsibility and a better salary. In 1968 she had been at her current job for eight years, getting advancements each year.

But she complained about the office politics and how the other women snickered when she told them she did not tell lies. Office politics were strange for her. She said she had always been honest, even when drinking, but "this office hanky-panky was new." She loved her work but admitted that nineteen years earlier she would not have had the serenity to take the office politics.

George finally got started again in his profession.

After eighteen years, they were both still very active in A.A. and doing a lot of twelfth step work. She expressed enormous gratitude to the fellowship for all it had given them. She said they were not reformed drunks, but informed alcoholics.

Like so many of us sober a long time, friends asked Ceil and George why they continued to go to meetings, do twelfth step work, and speak at other groups.

"They ask, 'Isn't eighteen years enough time to prove you have the alcoholic problem licked?' My answer is always the same: that I love my A.A. It is the one Fellowship that has given us our lives, freedom, and happiness. We are not reformed drunks—but informed alcoholics."

And she concludes: "I know to whom I owe my gratitude: my fellow members of A.A. I hope I shall never forget to be grateful."

She has been identified by one source as Ceil M., but her update was signed C.F. Perhaps that was a typo in the A.A. *Grapevine*, or perhaps she had begun using her maiden name for professional reasons, or perhaps she remarried after being divorced or widowed.

Those Golden Years

Cecil (Teet) C.

3rd ed. p. 327

"All the joys of retirement lay ahead for the movie publicist. Safely pensioned, with no job to protect, at last he could drink as he pleased."

Teet's date of sobriety, according to one source, was December 1970. He was 75 at the time his story was written.

Raised in Kansas, which was dry, he did not start drinking until he had finished college, done a stint on newspapers, married, become a father, and been in movie studio publicity two years.

At age thirty-two, and unaccustomed to drinking, he was assigned to keep media guests happy at a Halloween party given by a major star. At the party he got drunk and threw up and felt disgraced and humiliated. He vowed never to be embarrassed like that again, and though he continued to drink, he did it with caution when in public. Most of his heavy drinking was at home. (Not all hidden drunks, he points out, are housewives.)

He retired at sixty-eight, after forty years in public relations for Paramount Studios. He had successfully hidden his alcoholism until he retired. He had never lost a day's work because of drinking; never been warned about his drinking; had not lost his wife or family; had not lost his driver's license; had never been in jail or a barroom fight. He had managed to protect and maintain an image of respectability.

Now retired he was free to drink as much as he wanted. He lived with his wife who was a heart patient.

Teet pointed out that: "So long as a retiree woos his bottle at home, he stays out of public trouble. But for him, financial security or even affluence can be a tragedy."

When Teet retired, he said he would never be bored because he wanted to write novels, articles, short stories, and scripts on which he had copious notes. Creativity at the typewriter would keep him busy and alert, he thought.

He managed to sell a few things, but his writing career could be summed up in the couplet: "Alcohol gave me wings to fly/And then it took away the sky."

One day he remembered a line from an Alan Ladd movie, *Shane*, on which he had worked. "The trouble is, old man, you've lived too long."

Crises were emerging rapidly as he approached his seventieth birthday. Death seemed the only way out. But first he had to empty the upper cupboard full of empties so that they would not be found after his death. His sick wife, who didn't know the extent of his drinking, woke and caught him at it. She gasped and he feared she was having another heart attack.

This caused him to go into action. That evening he poured out the truth to her, admitting he was an alcoholic, and telling her that he would go to A.A. He attended his first A.A. meeting two nights later and never took another drink.

One advantage of those forty years as a movie press agent was that he had worked so long in a profession where fakery, deceit, and untruths are tools of the trade, he instantly recognized honesty when he heard it, from the mouths of A.A. members.

He had said he would not be bored in retirement. He was not. A.A. kept his retirement years full. Not long before he wrote his story, he lunched with another retired publicist who was close to tears in describing his boredom. Teet could not help thinking "You poor guy. I feel so sorry for you. You're not an alcoholic. You can never know the pure joy of recovery within the Fellowship of Alcoholics Anonymous."

Teet died on June 26, 1992.

The Housewife Who Drank at Home

Author unknown

2nd ed. p. 375; 3rd ed.; p. 335; 4th ed. p. 295

"She hid her bottles in clothes hampers and dresser drawers. She realized what she was becoming. In A.A., she discovered she had lost nothing and had found everything."

This story is of an alcoholic woman who stayed at home to care for her family. Her bar was her kitchen, her living room, her bedroom, the back bathroom, and the two hampers.

She had never been a very heavy social drinker, but during a period of particular stress and strain she resorted to alcohol in her home, alone, as a means of temporary release and a means of getting a little extra sleep. She didn't think a little wine would hurt her, but soon she was a chronic wine drinker. She needed it and couldn't live without it.

She became secretive about how much she drank. She pretended to be doing a lot of entertaining when she bought more wine, not wanting the clerk to know it was for herself.

When the doctor prescribed a little brandy for her son to help him through the night when he coughed, she switched from wine to brandy for three weeks. Soon she was in D.T.'s and screaming on the telephone for her mother and husband to come help her.

Thinking it would help if she got out of the house, she became active in civic affairs. As long as she worked she didn't drink but had to get back to that first drink somehow. While she was out of the house her behavior was fine, but her husband and children saw the other side of her. She had turned into a Jekyll-and-Hyde personality.

When the children were in school from nine to three, she started a little business and was fairly successful in it. But it was just a substitute for drink and she still needed that drink.

She tried switching to beer, which she had hated. Now she grew to love it and would drink it warm or cold.

Through all of this, her husband, whom she had turned against and treated badly, stayed with her and tried to help her.

Finally, a doctor recommended A.A. At one time the admission that she was an alcoholic meant shame, defeat, and failure to her. Now she was able to interpret that defeat, and that failure, and that shame, as seeds of victory. It was only through feeling defeat and feeling failure, the inability to cope with her life and with alcohol, that she was able to surrender and accept the fact that she had the disease of alcoholism and that she had to learn to live again without alcohol.

In A.A. she found that for the first time she could face her problems honestly and squarely. She took everything that A.A. had to give her. She surrendered. To her surrender brought with it the ability to run her home, to face her responsibilities, to take life as it comes day by day. She had surrendered once to the bottle and couldn't do those things.

She was brought up to believe in God, but not until she found A.A. did she know faith in the reality of God, the reality of His power that is now with her in everything she does.

Lifesaving Words

Trevor K., Lucknow, India

3rd ed. p. 342

"For this officer in the Indian Army, going on the wagon was not enough, attempts at control failed. The answer came to him by mail."

This man's sobriety date was October 24, 1957.

He attended high school in an American-sponsored Methodist public school, known as Philander Smith College, and eventually became a schoolmaster. He left that to join the Jat Regiment, one of the longest serving (over 200 years) and most decorated regiments of the Indian Army, where he rose to the rank of Lieutenant Colonel. It was after he joined the Army that his alcoholism made itself known.

Eight years before writing his story, he and his wife spent a vacation on a sixty-day leave in Naini Tal, the mountain resort. That was his first long vacation since joining the army. It was during this vacation that he decided to stop drinking, and he succeeded in this attempt for approximately fifteen months with only a couple of slips. But being an alcoholic, he always looked forward to the day when he could drink again.

At Christmas time the next year he convinced his wife that he had alcohol under control and could do controlled drinking over Christmas and the New Year. In a short time it became uncontrolled drinking. For the next three years he tried often again to stop but failed miserably.

Then he saw an A.A. advertisement in a newspaper and wrote to the address it gave. The reply came putting him in touch by mail with an A.A. member in New Delhi. This man sent him literature which he read systematically since then, and A.A. literature kept him sober. In November 1957, he registered as a "loner" due to his army postings.

Trevor's service postings took him all over India, so he became a roving ambassador of the A.A. movement, sowing the seeds of the fellowship at Bangalore, Kanpur, Lucknow, Allahabad, Calcutta and other cities.

The year before writing his story he took another vacation in Naini Tal. He made this one an A.A. vacation. He read, studied, and meditated on every bit of A.A. literature in his possession, studied the Big Book again, and took down notes for reference purposes.

"The difference between the two vacations was this: On the first, though on the water wagon, I looked forward to my next drink. I went on the wagon more to placate my wife than anything else. On the second, I knew—as I know now—that if I remained away from the first drink, then I had not to worry about the hundredth one. And I knew this: Once an alcoholic, always an alcoholic. I owe everything to A.A."

He died on December 31, 1986.

Physician Heal Thyself!

Dr. Earle M., San Francisco
Bay Area, California

2nd ed. p. 393, 3rd ed. p. 345, 4th ed. p. 301

"Psychiatrist and surgeon, he had lost his way until he realized that God, not he, was the Great Healer."

Earle had his last day of drinking and using drugs on June 15, 1953. An A.A. friend, Harry, took him to his first meeting the following week, the Tuesday Night Mill Valley A.A. group, which met in Wesley Hall at the Methodist Church. There were only five people there, all men: a butcher, a carpenter, a baker, and his friend Harry H., a mechanic/inventor. He loved A.A. from the start, and though he has been critical of the program at times, his devotion has remained constant.

Described in his story heading as a psychiatrist and surgeon, he was qualified in many fields. During his long career, he has been a prominent professor of obstetrics and gynecology, and an outstanding clinician at the University of California at San Francisco. He was a fellow of the American College of Surgeons and of the International College of Surgeons, a diplomate of the American Board of Obstetrics and Gynecology, board-certified psychiatrist, vice-president of the American Association of Marital and Family Therapists, and a lecturer on human sexuality.

He was raised in San Francisco, but was born on August 3, 1911, in Omaha, Nebraska, and lived there until he was ten. His parents were alcoholics. In Omaha they lived on the wrong side of the tracks, and he wore hand-me-down clothes from relatives. He was ashamed of this and could not begin to accept it until years later. He revealed none of this in his story. Instead, he talked about how successful he had been in virtually everything he had done. He said he lost nothing that most alcoholics lose and described his skid row as the skid row of success.

But in 1988 he wrote an autobiography which reveals much more of his story: Dr. Earle M., *Physician Heal Thyself! 35 Years of Adventures in Sobriety by an AA 'Old-Timer.'*

During his first year in A.A. he went to New York and met Bill W. They became very close and talked frequently both on the phone and in person. He frequently visited Bill at his home, Stepping Stones. He called Bill one of his sponsors and said there was hardly a topic they did not discuss in detail. He took a Fifth Step with Bill. And Bill often talked over his depressions with Earle.

In a search for serenity Earle studied and practiced many forms of religion: Hinduism, Buddhism, Taoism, Confucianism, and ancestor worship.

He has long been a strong advocate for the cross-addiction theory and predicted that over time we would see the evolution of Addictions Anonymous.

When he was sober about ten years, Earle developed resentments against newcomers and began a group in San Francisco for oldtimers. It was called The Forum. He wrote a credo for it, designed with ten steps for chemically dependent people. He felt that addiction represents a single disease with many open doors leading to it: alcohol, opiates, amphetamines, cocaine, etc. Most of the Forum members were also devoted A.A. members.

He also established a new kind of A.A. group, which used confrontational techniques. Some A.A. members disliked it intensely, while others seemed to gain a great deal from it.

Many alcoholics make geographic changes when they are drinking. But Earle seems to have made his after achieving sobriety. He has lived in many places, both in this country and abroad, traveled around the world three times, and attended A.A. everywhere he went. He also married several times.

In 1968 he divorced his first wife, Mary, whom he had married in 1940. She once told him she had great respect for him as a doctor, but none as a human being. He admitted that he'd had affairs during the marriage, even after joining A.A. His relationship with their only child, Jane, who was a very successful opera singer, was strained, but he gave her an opportunity to air her feelings in his book. She wrote that when she received the gold medallion at the International Tchaikovsky Voice Competition in Moscow in 1966, a high honor, her father did not attend. Some people told her that it was not easy for him to see her become such a success—to be so in the public eye. She added that their paths were still separate, but she did not ever totally close a door because he *was* her father.

In the 1960s he was experimenting with encounter and sensitivity awareness groups, which were then in vogue. At one of the encounter marathons he met his second wife, Katie, and within a year they were married and soon moved to Lake Tahoe. They lived separately except for two brief periods, and after a few years were divorced.

Later he accepted a job with the U.S. State Department at the University of Saigon Medical School, in Korea. He spent five years there, after which he returned to San Francisco, hoping to rekindle his marriage to Katie.

In September 1975 he moved to Hazard, Kentucky, to work at the Hazard Appalachian Regional Hospital. There he met his third wife, Freda, thirty years younger than he was. Freda came from a truly humble background. She was the daughter of a miner who had died of black lung disease. She and her six brothers were raised in a typical two-room coal miner's house in Hazard. During his relationship with her and her family he was able to put to rest some ghosts concerning his Nebraska background. This wonderful family helped him to re-evaluate his memories of Omaha.

In 1978 his feet began again to itch again. He accepted a short-term job in Nepal. When he was offered a long-term assignment, Freda and his stepsons did not want to leave Kentucky. Disappointed, he returned to Kentucky, and obtained work as a gynecologist in a family planning clinic, and also lectured to medical students on human sexuality at the University of Louisville Medical School. When he moved again, this time to Kirkland, Washington, Freda again refused to leave Kentucky. They were divorced soon after. They remained friendly and talked to one another on the phone about twice a year.

From all his travels, he always seemed to return to the San Francisco Bay Area. In 1980 he accepted a position as medical director of the Institute for Advanced Study of Human Sexuality in San Francisco. There he met his fourth wife, Mickey. She was a Ph.D. candidate at the Institute. He described her as a vibrant, open, honest, direct woman without pretense, non-threatening, sexually on fire, lacking in prejudice, and tolerant about all aspects of life— including human sexuality. She was already an Al-Anon member when they met, having been married to an alcoholic. She also made contributions in the field of alcoholism and recovery at Merritt Peralta Chemical Dependence Recovery Hospital in Oakland, California. They married and remained together until her death in 2000. His book is dedicated to her.

In a conversation in July 2001, Earle said that he still got to an A.A. meeting almost every day. His eyesight was not too good, he reported, but otherwise he was full of vim and vigor. From his voice, one would have taken him for a man of 40.

He died on January 13, 2003, at the age of 91, forty-nine years sober.

A Teen-ager's Decision

Lisa, Washington State

3rd ed. p. 353

"Just three years of drinking pushed a shy, lonely young girl to the depths of depression. Out of sheer despair, she called for help."

Lisa's story was first named "The Story of Lisa" in an early printing of "Young People and A.A."

She began to drink at fifteen, and never drank socially, but always as often and as much as she could. She wanted to drink herself to death. It seemed that her whole life had been spent on the outside looking in. She had been unhappy, lonely, and scared for so long that when she discovered alcohol it seemed to be the answer to all her problems.

But it became a painful answer as hangovers, blackouts, trouble, and remorse set in. She recounted driving her parents' car down a bank, ramming the steel fence around someone's backyard. She was informed the next morning that she had not behaved like her shy, quiet self. She remembers lying on a cold cement floor shredding into little bits several pieces of stolen identification cards and washing her face in the toilet bowl trying to sober up and screaming hysterically while clinging to bars too high to see out of and cursing everyone that came near her.

She lost her driver's license and became a ward of the court and was put on probation. None of this impressed her.

Thinking that school was interfering with her drinking, she ran away from home, despite the fact that she was near graduation and her mother was sick in a hospital.

She recounts hitchhiking with a friend to Las Vegas from Washington State, spending a month drinking, taking drugs, and finding shelter where they could and accepting meals from anyone, begging and stealing anything they needed. They were arrested and her friend was institutionalized for eight months. But Lisa had turned eighteen during the trip, and so was allowed to return home to a pair of miserable, hurt parents.

She began to hate herself and drank primarily to ease her conscience and forget. But things got progressively worse. Finally, she began to take a good look at herself: she had managed to drink her way through all her friends, had no one in the world to talk to, and was increasing guilt-ridden and depressed. She was too weak to continue this day-by-day suicide.

Thank God she knew of A.A. and called. She had no idea what would happen, she just knew she didn't want to live if life was going to go on like it was.

At the time she wrote her story she was counting her blessings instead of her troubles. A.A. became a way of life and living for her. It brought about a revelation of self, the discovery of an inner being, and awareness of God. She wouldn't give it up or trade it for anything. And knows "the only one who can take it away from me is me—by taking that first drink."

Rum, Radio and Rebellion

Pete W., Pittsburgh, Pennsylvania

2nd ed. p. 317, 3rd ed. p. 356

"This man faced the last ditch when his wife's voice from 1,300 miles away sent him to A.A."

One source said of Pete that his original date of sobriety was June 1944, but he slipped briefly in September of 1944. However, in an update of his story which was printed in the A.A. *Grapevine* in January 1968, he says that he came into A.A. in 1945.

Pete was fifty-three years of age when he wrote his story, with over nine years of A.A. behind him.

He was born in Cleveland, Ohio, he says in this story in the Big Book, the only child of a prominent dentist and a very proud mother. He had every advantage: private schools, dancing schools, two colleges, raccoon coats, automobiles, and a listing in the social register. All this resulted in a very popular but spoiled brat.

He ran away from school to join the army in World War I, but the Armistice was signed the very day he arrived in Atlanta to sign up.

He ran out of money and wired his father for funds to come home, but his father wired back saying he could stay there until he earned enough to get home. It took him a year.

He went to work in Birmingham for a newspaper at fifteen dollars a week. During Prohibition he had his first taste of moonshine. For the next twenty-five years he drank anything and everything at the slightest excuse.

When he made it home in 1920, he re-entered school and did a year's work in three months, proving that he could do it when he wanted to.

During the roaring '20s, he drank a great deal and thought he was having a grand time. He got to Europe for a few weeks, had cards entitling him to an entrée in the better joints between Cleveland and New York, got married, and built a home in a fashionable suburb of Cleveland. This high living ended with the 1929 stock market crash. In a couple of years, he lost his worldly goods, and his wife left him.

He then made a geographic cure to New York. He began working in the broadcasting business. He worked for a Chicago firm that represented several large radio stations. It was his job to sell time on these stations to advertising agencies in New York.

Then he met a woman he wanted to marry, but she refused him at first. He persisted. In January 1938 he took a job managing a small radio station in Vermont, and again proposed to the girl. She was then working in Salt Lake City, but said if he would curtail his drinking she would consider marrying him. They were married in Montreal in November 1938. But on their first Christmas he came home drunk.

In 1940 they moved to Pittsburgh where he managed two radio stations under the same ownership. His wife tried everything she could to help him, but by early spring of 1944, his drinking had become so troublesome that she left him and moved to her parents' home in Florida. She told him she was not leaving because she didn't love him, but because she did love him and could not bear to be there when he lost the respect of others and, above all, of his own self-respect.

Full of self-pity he staggered home one day determined to kill himself. "Then, by George, she'd be sorry!" But he passed out, and when he woke, looking straight at him was a large oil painting of his wife, he remembered her words: "I'm not leaving you because I don't love you, but because I love you." This was about ten p.m. The precise time is important, because he found out later that it corresponded with something his wife was doing at that same time in Florida, many miles away.

Then, in spite of the late hour, he called AA, and within a couple of hours two people from AA had come to his home and were explaining the program to him. After a few AA meetings he drove to

Florida unannounced and showed his wife the AA literature he had brought with him to convince her that he was trying to change. She returned with him to Pittsburgh.

In September he went to New York alone and got drunk. It was a one-day drunk and he didn't tell anyone. He began skipping meetings. On New Year's Day he almost took a drink but did not. It frightened him and he started going back to meetings. He met an old friend new in AA, and full of enthusiasm. This fired his spirits again, and he started really working the program. Then, when the group was celebrating his one years of sobriety, he told the truth. It had only been nine months since his last drink. He had thrown off the big lie that had been burdening him for months. "What a wonderful relief."

His first spiritual experience came early. While in Florida trying to convince his wife that he was serious about A.A., she picked up a clipping from the *St. Petersburg Times* about A.A. She had considered sending it to him. She cut out that clipping at about ten o'clock on the same night, and at the same time as he called A.A. in Pittsburgh, some 1300 miles away.

Pete wrote an update of his story for the January 1968 issue of the A.A. *Grapevine* entitled "No Graduation from AA!" In this updated version, he said that when he came to A.A. he believed in God, but that was about the limit of his spiritual qualifications. He was in the program about three years before he found comfort and deep satisfaction in prayer. Insight came gradually through the voices of oldtimers.

When he and his wife moved to a new neighborhood in Pittsburgh, several ministers called on them asking them to visit their churches. It was embarrassing to his wife when the ministers groped around to find out just what their religion was. One young minister came quickly to the point by asking his wife what religion her husband followed. Without hesitancy she said, Alcoholics Anonymous. The minister replied that he knew of no better one. Pete went on to say that A.A. is not a religion, but certainly is a spiritual program.

He expressed dismay that responsibility to our group, to A.A. as a whole, and especially to General Services, is a subject dwelt upon far too lightly by many of our members. He said it distresses him particularly when older members gradually drop out of the picture. We need their good experience, and they should be grateful enough to carry on the message as their responsibility to the future of Alcoholics Anonymous and, in many instances, to their very own sobriety. He hated to meet members who consider that they have graduated from A.A. They are missing so much! Pete knows now, he said in this little article, that sobriety is not a destination, but an endless journey—and, he hastened to add, a very beautiful journey.

This 1968 update said that it was written in Cleveland, Tennessee, a little town which had a population of only 20,000 at the time. Did the *Grapevine* confuse that town with Cleveland, Ohio, or otherwise make a mistake here?

Any Day Was Washday

Author unknown

3rd ed. p. 369

"This secret drinker favored the local Laundromat as a watering hole. Now, she no longer risks losing her home, her self-respect, or her laundry."

One source says this woman's date of sobriety was April 1973.

Her father was a big Irish oilman who came up through the "school of hard knocks" and so had to be a two-fisted drinker. Her sweet mother said he had a "weakness." The author realized that something was wrong and developed a great sense of insecurity.

She married at nineteen and had six children. In the beginning she and her husband drank on social occasions, but without problems.

Then a series of tragedies occurred. Her father died from falling down a flight of stairs while drunk; after his death her sweet mother took up drinking and died of cirrhosis of the liver; and then her five-year-old girl was killed by a neighbor's car. She couldn't take all the stress and was soon admitted to a state hospital for the mentally ill. After a few months she was "released and left the world of insanity, only to return to the world of alcoholic insanity."

Her husband disapproved of her drinking so she would gather up the soiled clothes and go the Laundromat, buying alcohol on the way. She would get drunk at the Laundromat, lose shirts, and once lost the entire wash. (During this time she was considering doing laundry for the neighbors as a part-time job, so that she could spend all her time at the Laundromat.)

Finally, her husband decided he wanted a divorce and told her to leave because she was "unfit as a mother, a wife, and a laundress."

Fortunately, her sister-in-law knew of a place that helped alcoholic women, a halfway house. There she found A.A. and learned that she didn't have a "weakness" but the disease of alcoholism.

One night, a few weeks after joining the Fellowship, she was surprised and delighted to see a familiar face—her husband. It is unclear whether he was there because he, too, was an alcoholic, or whether it was an open meeting that he attended to learn about the disease in order to help her. She says only "he was learning, too."

They resumed their marriage, moved away from the street of sad memories, and found a new home. But for her, what is more important is "I found a new life in Alcoholics Anonymous. I'm very active in A.A. work and active at home, too, with my family. I still wash clothes, lots of them, but I no longer lose them at the Laundromat. That's right! During three years in A.A., I haven't lost so much as one shirt."

It Might Have Been Worse

Chet R.

2nd ed. p. 382, 3rd ed. p. 373, 4th ed. p. 348

"Alcohol was a looming cloud in this banker's bright sky. With rare foresight he realized it could become a tornado."

Chet's sobriety date and place of entry into A.A. are unknown.

He was raised in a family of modest circumstances, in a small town in the Midwest. He attended public schools, worked part-time after school and during vacations, and participated in some athletics. But ambition to succeed was instilled in him by his Scandinavian parents who had come to this country because they thought there were better opportunities here.

Wartime service in the Army in World War I interrupted his plans for success. After the war he continued his education, married and had a family, and got started in business.

He worked hard and in time became an officer and director of a large commercial bank, and also became a director in many important institutions.

His drinking did not start until he was thirty-five and fairly successful in his career, but success brought increased social activities which involved alcohol. At first it was just an occasional drink, then the "nineteenth hole" at the golf course, then cocktail hours. Eventually the increased drinking substituted for what he really enjoyed doing. Golf, hunting, and fishing became excuses to drink excessively.

He made promises and broke them many times; went on the wagon and fell off; tried psychiatry but gave the psychiatrist no cooperation. Blackouts, personality changes, hangovers and remorse resulted in his living in constant fear. He thought no one knew the extent of his drinking and was surprised to learn later than that everyone knew. His wife tried to control the amount he drank and tried leaving or threatening to leave. Nothing seemed to work.

After a drunk which ruined his wife's birthday party, his daughter said, "It's Alcoholics Anonymous—or else!"

A lawyer in A.A. called on him the next day, spent most of the day with him, and took him to his first meeting that night.

At first, he wondered if he belonged in A.A. because he hadn't had the experience of jails, lost jobs, and lost families that he heard others describe. But the answer was in the first step. Most certainly he was powerless over alcohol, and for him his life had become unmanageable. It wasn't how far he had gone, but where he was headed. He was wise enough to recognize that.

He began to realize how his obsession with alcohol had led to self-pity, resentments, dishonest thinking, prejudice, ego, a critical and antagonistic attitude toward anyone and everyone who dared to cross him, and vanity. It took him some time to realize that the Twelve Steps were designed to help correct these defects of character and so help remove the obsession to drink.

A willingness to do whatever he was told to do simplified the program for him. He was told to study the AA book, not just read it, to go to meetings, and to get active.

He was desperately in earnest to follow through and understand what was expected of him as a member of A.A. and to take each Step of the Twelve as rapidly as possible.

The fact that AA is a spiritual program didn't scare him or raise any prejudice in his mind. He couldn't afford that luxury. He had tried his way and had failed.

When he joined A.A. he did so for the sole purpose of getting sober and staying sober. But he found it was so much more. A new and different outlook on life started opening up almost immediately. Each day seemed to be so much more productive and satisfying. He got so much more enjoyment out of living and found an inner pleasure in simple things.

Above all, he was grateful to A.A. for his sobriety, which meant so much to his family, friends and business associates, because God and A.A. were able to do for him something he was unable to do for himself.

A Flower of the South

Esther E., Houston, Texas

2nd ed. p. 343, 3rd ed. p. 384

"Somewhat faded, she nevertheless bloomed afresh. She still had her husband, her home, and a chance to help start A.A. in Texas."

Esther's date of sobriety was May 16, 1941.

She was a very attractive woman, full of pep. She was raised in New Orleans where social drinking was acceptable. At home they always had wine with dinner and cordials after dinner. She attended cocktail parties, dances and nightclubs.

The first time she realized what alcohol could do for her was her own wedding. She was so afraid that everything wouldn't be perfect that she became very nervous and "was really in a terrific state" when her father said "Miss Esther is about to faint. Get her something to drink." The servant came back with a water glass full of bourbon and made her drink it down. The bourbon hit as she started down the aisle. "I walked down that aisle just like May West in her prime. I wanted to do it all over again," she wrote.

From that day on she used alcohol to ease social situations and didn't know when she crossed over the line into alcoholism.

She divorced her husband after seven years and went home to her parents but couldn't stand living with them and went back to Texas and remarried her ex-husband. Then they moved to Oklahoma. The drinking got worse; her husband would come home day after day to find her passed out. She was sent to a mental hospital where they kept her seventeen days.

When they moved to Houston the drinking continued. She went out one day to walk the dog. A patrol car passed and saw her staggering and stopped to take her home, but she got "sassy" with him so he took the dog home and took poor Esther to jail. She was only there a few hours. When her husband came to get her the look of disgust on his face helped her to hit bottom.

He had read a story about A.A. in the *Saturday Evening Post* a few weeks before. He finally showed it to her with the ultimatum: "If you will try this thing, I'll go along with you. If you don't, you will have to go home. I cannot sit by and watch you destroy yourself!"

She wrote to the GSO office in New York. Within a week a letter came back with A.A. literature. It was the routine letter they sent everyone, but with it was a handwritten letter from Ruth Hock, A.A.'s non-alcoholic secretary. That personal touch did a lot to help Esther.

Esther was full of gratitude to her husband, and to A.A. members who had paved the way for her.

During her second year in A.A. they were transferred to Dallas and started an A.A. group there in 1943. The telephone number in Dallas that Ruth Hock had given her had been disconnected when she arrived. But undaunted, she started seeking other alcoholics to twelfth step.

Esther had lived in Dallas from 1927 to 1932 and, according to a letter she wrote to New York dated March 29, 1943, "This is where I had been so sick for five years. Where I started trying out all the doctors, hospitals and cures (the Sanitarium three times) so I've lots to do. First off, four doctors to call on and let them look over 'exhibit A' (me)! My minister (Episcopal) has two prospects for us. He tried so hard to help me for years, had never heard of A.A." She added "Hope I have much A.A. to report in my next letter. You'll be hearing from me!" They did indeed.

A week later, April 5, she wrote "Dear Bobbie [Margaret R. Burger, Bill's secretary at the time]: The new Dallas Group met for their first time last night! Three inactive alkies, one active from Detroit and two non-alcoholics who brought the active one." The group met for some time in Esther's home.

Esther died on June 3, 1960, with slightly more than 19 years of sobriety. Her copy of the Big Book, which is signed by Bill W., is on display in the Dallas Central Office.

Calculating the Costs

Author unknown

3rd ed. p. 396

"A retired Navy man looks back over twenty years of drinking, to add up his A.A. 'initiation fee.'"

This man's sobriety date is unknown. But since he likes calculations let us do some calculating, based on what he tells us in his story, to find out when he came into A.A.

If he entered the Navy at the age of twenty-one, not long after the United States entered World War II, say early 1942, and served twenty years in the Navy, he would have been forty-one when he retired in 1962. The heading on his story refers to twenty years of drinking, but in the third paragraph of the story the figure he himself gives is twenty-five years of drinking. He says he started serious drinking at eighteen, so he must have entered A.A. two years after getting out of the Navy, i.e., about 1964.

Lack of funds and young age kept him from drinking much before the age of eighteen, but he was quite inventive. Beginning when he was fourteen he displayed alcoholic tendencies. He started to steal wine from the family jug, siphoning it off one drink at a time so it wouldn't be missed, and saving it up until he had about a pint so that he could get drunk. "Even at that age," he says, "I had learned that one drink was not enough. I had to have enough to get drunk on, or what was the use?"

He points out that his initiation fee was at least $10,000. All alcoholics pay a high initiation fee to enter A.A. But as this alcoholic points out, "Incalculable are the intangible initiation fees that A.A. members have paid, the sick, sick hangovers, the remorse, guilt, broken homes, jails, and institutions, and the mental anguish in general that has been generated over the years."

Stars Don't Fall

Countess Felicia G., New York City

2nd ed. p. 401, 3rd ed. p. 400

"A titled lady, she still saw her world darkening. When the overcast lifted, the stars were there as before."

Felicia entered A.A. in 1943 and relapsed briefly during the first year. Her last drink was in 1944. Marty M. ("Women Suffer Too") was her sponsor.

She was born in 1905, in the family castle in Poland, the daughter of Count Josef G. and Eleanor Medill "Cissy" Patterson, editor of the *Washington Times*. Cissy was also a cousin of Robert McCormick of the *Chicago Tribune*.

Because of the Count's violent, abusive behavior, when Felicia was about two years old Cissy fled with her to London. The Count followed them and succeeded in literally kidnapping his daughter and taking her back to Poland. For two years he parked her in a convent to be cared for by the nuns. Then, through the intervention of President Taft, four-year-old Felicia was returned to Cissy in a dramatic event that riveted the attention of the world's press.

Felicia believed her alcoholic problem began long before she drank. Her personality from the time she could remember anything was "the perfect set-up for an alcoholic career." She was always out of step with the world, her family, with people in general. She lived in a dream world.

Until her early thirties, when her drinking became a problem, she lived in large houses, with servants and all the luxuries that she could possibly want. But she never felt she belonged.

Felicia was married three times, first in 1925 to Drew Pearson, the young newspaperman whom she mentions on page 402. He eventually became a nationally famous radio commentator and author of the "Washington Merry-Go-Round" newspaper column. She divorced him three years later.

She met him again when she had been sober ten years and he told her he had always felt guilty because she became an alcoholic after their divorce. She was able to explain that she would have become an alcoholic anyway, that she had been a sick person, unfit for marriage.

She married Dudley de Lavigne in 1934 (the husband mentioned on page 493) but was again divorced less than a year later. She was married again after her recovery, to John Kennedy Magruder, whom she married in 1958 and divorced in 1964. For most of her professional career she went by the name of Felicia G.

Through her first two marriages, and several geographic cures in Europe, her drinking caused more and more degradation. By 1943 she had moved to New York and was living a Bohemian life in the Village. Her daughter, Ellen, was taken away from her during this period.

Felicia sank lower and lower, but eventually had the good fortune to find a new analyst, Dr. Ruth Fox (who later became the medical director of the National Council on Alcoholism). Dr. Fox told her about A.A., gave her the Big Book, and finally persuaded her to meet with Bill W. Bill arranged for her to meet Marty M. (Marty told how Bill called and said "I have a dame down here whose name I can't pronounce. I don't know what to do with her.")

The woman who answered the door at Marty's apartment (page 413) was Marty's long term partner, Priscilla P., a very glamorous art director at *Vogue* magazine. Felicia speaks of Priscilla on page 414. They took Felicia to her first AA meeting and Felicia and Priscilla became lifelong friends. Marty was sponsor to them both.

When Marty spoke at Felicia's sixteenth anniversary celebration, she joked about how at their first meeting Felicia said little. But Marty talked on and on about her own history. Finally, Felicia admitted she drank a little too, "not much—once in a while. Nothing very serious, you understand."

It was a long time before Marty heard the full story. Little by little episodes came out that were not so mild. "I remember as though it were yesterday the first time I heard about her fighting ability." She turned to Felicia and asked: "What was it they used to call you?" Felicia replied, "Sadie, the fighting Pollock."

It wasn't until after Felicia had a slip that she dropped her defenses and started to really talk about what alcohol had done in her life.

She was a talented writer and—with Marty and Priscilla—helped start the A.A. *Grapevine.* She also kept journals, one of them entitled "To Those Who Didn't Make It." In this journal she describes Marty's form of sponsorship. She called Marty from a bar expecting Marty to run to her rescue. Instead, Marty said "Well, honey, what can I do about it?" Marty didn't let her dramatize herself.

Felicia wrote an update of her story for the November 1967 *Grapevine*. It was signed "F. M., New Canaan, Connecticut." In it she said she was disappointed to learn that her story would be in the section labeled "They Stopped in Time." She thought she had sunk pretty low.

Felicia celebrated her 55th anniversary of sobriety in 1998. That same year she gave an interview about her friend Marty M. to Marty's biographers. During the interview she was unable to communicate more than five minutes at a time before she would fall asleep in her chair. Her grandson, who was present, said it was a pity they hadn't come six months earlier, when her mind was still clear. But they were given access to Felicia's journals (1950-1988).

A few months later, on February 26, 1999, Felicia died at the age of 92.

Growing Up All Over Again

Harris K., Illinois

3rd ed. p. 418

"A 'good boy' reached adulthood and success without achieving maturity or fulfillment. Defeated by alcohol and pills, he found the way to a new life."

Harris's date of sobriety is believed to be 1960.

He was a second-generation A.A. member, taken to A.A. by a woman whom his father had taken to A.A. thirteen years earlier.

He neither drank nor smoked until he was nineteen years old. He was an honor graduate in high school, and the "good boy" to whom mothers pointed when their sons went astray. He was awarded a scholarship to a famous old eastern college but began to drink at the end of his freshman year. By the junior year he had to transfer to an easier state university to keep his grades up.

He entered dental school, his admission, oddly enough, arranged by the dentist who started A.A. in Amarillo, Texas. During his first year there, he married.

He went through dental school sober for the most part, except that he imitated his father's periodic drinking pattern by getting drunk at a few parties and on vacation. He graduated with honors but could feel no real responsibility as a father or a husband.

Then he served a four-year tour in the Navy, two of which were spent in the Philippines. He described his life there as "a nightmare of periodic binges on alcohol and pills, adultery, unhappy hours at the dental office, seeing my wife give birth to our second child and have several miscarriages, living in a turbulent household, and making continual attempts to be the respectable dentist, husband, father, and community leader."

His return to the United States proved effective as a geographical cure, and he was sober for a while, with the help of the church. He had another brief period of sobriety when he went back to his hometown to go into private practice, but it did not take long for the pressures to bring out his immaturity and his insecurity.

By the age of twenty-eight he was well established and had been elected president of a civic club, was a deacon and a Sunday school teacher, and had a lovely wife and three children. His wife was in the Junior League, and he was on the board of directors of the local center for the mentally retarded. But he had a queasy feeling in the pit of his stomach, which hinted to him that everything was phony. He had no real peace of mind, nor any gratitude.

In less than two years he had lost his practice, his home, his wife and children. He tried the church and psychiatry and finally came to A.A. He was twenty-nine when he had his last drunk. During that last drunk, which lasted four days, he threatened to kill his children, beat his wife at home and on the church steps, mistreated a child in his office, and ran to a hospital for mental illness to avoid jail.

He came to A.A. simply because there were no other doors of help open to him in his hometown.

After coming to A.A. he was divorced, lost his practice, was legally restrained from seeing his children, went broke, and the dental society threatened him with the loss of his license. Only A.A. kept him from running away.

He went to meetings frequently, listened to tapes and attended A.A. conferences, worked on the Twelve Steps and with other alcoholics and their families.

A.A. gave him a new wife who was also an A.A. member, a beautiful stepdaughter, a new practice, a new home, and a new relationship with his four children. Most important, it enabled him to go back and start growing up all over again in all areas of his life.

He asks at the end of his story, "Why am I alive, free, a respected member of my community?" And he answers his own question: "Because A.A. really works for me!"

Unto the Second Generation

Author unknown, Chicago, Illinois

2nd ed. p. 355, 3rd ed. p. 422

"A young veteran tells how a few rough experiences pushed him into A.A.—and how he was therefore spared years of suffering."

This man's date of sobriety is believed to be February 1950.

He began drinking at about fifteen. In high school all the students had lockers in which they kept books, pencils, paper, gym equipment, etc. He did too, but he also kept beer in his locker. At sixteen he graduated to the "hard stuff." When the other kids went out to hamburger huts or ice cream parlors, pizza joints or bowling alleys after football games and dances, he headed for saloons where he could get drinks.

He worked after school pumping gas until ten or eleven at night. He tried to imitate the men he worked with by talking out of the side of his mouth as they did. He smoked as much, tried to drink as much, and do everything they did, only more so. He boosted his income by filching money from the Coke machine, short-sticking customers on oil, and selling oil he'd drained out of other cars.

He quit school when he was just past sixteen, already with a drinking problem. His parents both drank excessively and were getting progressively worse. He wanted love and affection from his parents but didn't get it so did what he pleased most of the time.

He and another boy ran away to Omaha from his home in Chicago. They broke into a church to find a place to sleep and accidentally set the church on fire. He spent the next three days in jail. His father, a newspaperman, had meanwhile filed a missing person report on him. He was identified and put on a train back to

Chicago. He went to work for the newspaper that employed his father and began dating a girl he worked with.

Nearly eighteen, he enlisted in the Navy to escape the Army draft. The night before he left for active duty he had planned to stay home, but his parents were drunk so he spent the night with his girlfriend and got very drunk himself. He was drunk when he was sworn in next morning, and drunk when he was discharged three years later.

At Great Lakes Boot Camp, he landed a soft job which exempted him from ordinary recruit training activities. Although he wasn't allowed visitors for the first eight weeks, his dad pulled some strings and his parents managed to visit him after three weeks. They smuggled in a couple of pints for him, but he'd already made connections to get a regular supply of alcohol.

When stationed at Pearl Harbor he managed to be allowed to live in the photo lab where he worked, and to get a constant supply of alcohol. The result was that he woke up one day in a hospital. The doctor told him he had been brought into the hospital "like a madman, crying, raving, ranting, swearing, completely in the throes of delirium tremens. The diagnosis was acute alcoholism.

At the court martial that followed he received only thirty days confinement, fifteen in solitary.

Two months later he was sent back to the States to be discharged. When the plane landed in San Diego he headed for Tijuana where he landed in jail for being drunk and causing a brawl. He was escorted back to San Diego the next morning by the Shore Patrol but was discharged on schedule.

His parents in the meantime had joined A.A. and he found them quite different from the parents he had known. "They had color in their faces, sparkle in their eyes and love in their hearts. It was a glorious homecoming." His Dad poured him welcome home drinks, not knowing how serious his drinking problem had become.

His drinking continued and when he had a second experience with D.T.'s he knew he was licked. He had packed more drinking into seven years than most people do in a lifetime.

The doctor in Hawaii had told him if he didn't stop drinking, he wouldn't live five years. He knew he had to stop. He didn't want to break his parents' hearts and maybe jeopardize their own carefully built up and hard-fought-for sobriety.

Though the red carpet had been rolled out for him, it wasn't easy. His new girlfriend called it quits a week after his decision to join A.A. Three days later he lost his job. The combination nearly threw him, but he attended meetings, talked to his folks and the younger people they had put him in contact with, and he stayed sober.

He joined A.A. at the age of twenty-two. He wrote his story when he was twenty-six. He said even if he were to revert to drinking, he still wouldn't give anything for the four years in A.A. They had been the happiest of his life. He had been helped morally, spiritually, mentally and materially through A.A. He used to think "Why live without whiskey?" Now he knew he couldn't live without A.A.

Four years earlier he had "nothing but a jumbled, mad existence." When he wrote his story, he had all anyone could ask. He had a lovely wife who understood his problems and tried to help him; two wonderful little boys; a good job; and kind and sympathetic parents. He was buying his house and owed no one—except A.A.

Fiona Dodd, The Big Book Stories

Me an Alcoholic?

Author unknown

2nd ed. p. 419, 3rd ed. p. 432, 4th ed. p. 382

"Barleycorn's wringer squeezed this author—but he escaped quite whole."

This author's date of sobriety is believed to be November 1947.

He reveals little of his childhood years or his origin, just the hint when discussing his seven years in psychotherapy that someone had coddled him and built him up, and then turned and beat him savagely.

He was a father, husband, homeowner, athlete, artist, musician, author, editor, aircraft pilot, and world traveler. He was listed in "Who's Who in America." He had been successful in the publishing business, his opinions were quoted in *Time* and *Newsweek* magazines with pictures, and he addressed the public by radio and television.

He drank heavily as was common in the literary circles in which he traveled. "Evening cocktails were as standard as morning coffee," and his average daily consumption ran a little more or less than a pint. This did not seem to affect his work. He was never drunk on the job, never missed a day's work, was seldom rendered totally ineffective by a hangover and kept his liquor expenses well within his adequate budget. How could he possibly be an alcoholic?

But he occasionally went on binges, usually one-night stands. In twenty-five years of drinking there were only a few occasions when he took a morning drink. He usually had excuses for the binges and tried several methods of controlling his drinking. These plans seemed to work for short periods.

Inwardly unhappy he turned to psychoanalysis. He spent seven years and ten thousand dollars on psychiatric care and emerged in worse condition than ever, although he learned a lot about himself, which would be useful later. His binges got closer and closer together and with more and more disastrous results. Soon he was in suicidal despair.

After his last binge, during which he did considerable damage to his home, he crawled back to his analyst and told him he thought he was an alcoholic.

His doctor agreed. He said he hadn't told him because he hadn't been sure until recently—the line between a heavy drinker and an alcoholic is not always clear—and that he wouldn't have believed him had he told him. The doctor admitted that there was nothing he could do for him, and that there was nothing medicine could do for him. But he suggested A.A.

Many times, in the years that followed the author thanked God for that doctor, a man who had the courage to admit failure and the humility to confess that all the hard-won learning of his profession could not turn up the answer.

In A.A. he found the power he needed. In the seven years since he had come to A.A. he had not had a drink.

He still had some hell to go through. His tower of worldly success collapsed, his alcoholic associates fired him, took control, and ran the enterprise into bankruptcy. His alcoholic wife took up with someone else and divorced him, taking with her all his remaining property.

But the most terrible blow was when his sixteen-year-old son was tragically killed. "The Higher Power was on deck to see me through, sober. I think He's on hand to see my son through, too. I think He's on hand to see all of us through whatever may come to us."

Some wonderful things had happened, too. His new wife and he didn't own any property to speak of and the flashy successes of another day were gone. But they had a baby "who, if you'll pardon a little post-alcoholic sentimentality, is right out of Heaven." His work was on a much deeper and more significant level than it ever was before, and he was, at the time he wrote his story, a fairly creative, relatively sane human being. "And should I have more bad times," he wrote, "I know that I'll never again have to go through these alone."

Acceptance Was the Answer

Dr. Paul O., M.D.,
Laguna Niguel, California

Titled DOCTOR, ALCOHOLIC, ADDICT
in 3rd ed., renamed for the 4th edition

3rd ed. p. 439; 4th ed. p. 407

"The physician wasn't hooked, he thought—he just prescribed drugs medically indicated for his many ailments. Acceptance was his key to liberation."

Paul's story is one of the most frequently quoted in the 3rd edition because it talks so much about acceptance (pages 449-450).

His original date of sobriety was December 1966, but he slipped until July 1967. He didn't think he was an alcoholic, he just had problems. "If you had my problems you'd drink too." His major problem was his wife. "If you had my wife you'd drink, too." He and his wife, Max, had been married twenty-eight years when he entered A.A. He said she was a natural Al-Anon long before they heard of either A.A. or Al-Anon.

His story in the Big Book, and tapes of his talks, show that Paul had a great sense of humor, and was a very humble man.

Paul had begun to drink when in pharmacy school to help him sleep. He went through pharmacy school, graduate school, medical school, internship, residency and specialty training, and finally went into practice. All the time his drinking kept increasing. Soon he began taking drugs to pep him up and tranquilizers to level off.

On occasion he tried to stop completely but had convulsions from withdrawal. When he went to Mayo Clinic he was put in the locked ward. Another hospitalization was in the psychiatric ward of a hospital where he was on the staff. But there he was introduced to A.A.

It took him a while to get off the alcohol and pills, but when he wrote his story he said: "Today, I find I can't work my A.A. program while taking pills, nor may I even have them around for dire emergencies only. I can't say 'Thy will be done,' and take a pill. I can't say, 'I'm powerless over alcohol, but solid alcohol is okay.' I can't say 'God could restore me to sanity but until He does, I'll control myself—with pills.'"

He started Pills Anonymous and Chemical Dependency Anonymous, but did not attend them because he got all he needed from A.A. He did not introduce himself as an alcoholic and addict and was irritated by people who want to broaden A.A. to include other addictions.

He wrote an article for the *Grapevine* on why doctors shouldn't prescribe pills for alcoholics, and because he had a dual problem was asked to write his story for the Big Book. It was originally published in the A.A. Grapevine with the title "Bronzed Moccasins" and an illustration of a pair of bronze moccasins. It was eventually renamed and included in the Big Book. His book, *There's More to Quitting Drinking than Quitting Drinking*, was published in 1995 by Sabrina Publishing, Laguna Niguel, California.

Paul complained in an interview with the A.A. Grapevine that the story might have "overshot the mark." One of the most uncomfortable things for him was the people who run up to him at a meeting and tell him how glad they are the story is in the book. "They say they were fighting with their home group because their home group won't let them talk about drugs. So they show their group the story and they say, 'By God, now you'll have to let me talk about drugs.' And I really hate to see the story as a divisive thing. I don't think we came to A.A. to fight each other."

But he denied that there is anything in the story he would want to change. The story "makes clear the truth that an alcoholic can also be an addict, and indeed that an alcoholic has a constitutional right to have as many problems as he wants! But that doesn't mean that every A.A. meeting has to be open to a discussion of drugs if it doesn't want to. Every meeting has the right to say it doesn't want drugs discussed. People who want to discuss drugs have other places where they can go to talk about that."

How did he work his program? "Pretty much every morning, before I get out of bed, I say the Serenity Prayer, the Third Step Prayer, and the Seventh Step Prayer. Then Max and I repeat those prayers along with other prayers and meditations at breakfast."

He had a special meeting format for early morning meetings. He called them Attitude Adjustment Meetings. They consisted largely of readings from the Big Book, prayers from the Big Book and 12 & 12, and a short session of positive pitches. The meetings were at 6:30 a.m. or 7:00 a.m. each day.

Paul died on May 19, 2000. Max died on July 1, 2001.

THEY LOST NEARLY ALL

A Five-Time Loser Wins

Morris B., Long Island, New York

3rd ed. p. 457

"The worst of prison treatment couldn't break this tough con. He was serving time on his fifth felony conviction when a miracle happened."

Morris said that, like most alcoholics, for him it was "Eat, drink and be merry, for tomorrow you die." But he couldn't die. He kept painfully awakening each time, mentally, physically, and spiritually, sick.

There are worse things than dying, he points out, "but is there any death worse than the progressive, self-induced, slow suicide of the practicing alcoholic?"

Morris described himself as a five-time loser and explained that this means that he had five felony convictions (not including the cases beaten). He served time in four penitentiaries and several prison camps, including a maximum-security camp. He spent eleven months in solitary confinement, bouncing in and out of the "hole" (a bare concrete-and-steel cubicle) about five times during those eleven months. The crimes that he committed were the result of drinking and using drugs.

Even in prison he was always fighting the system, even to the extent of using his body: he cracked his leg with a sixteen-pound sledgehammer in the rock hole; he let lye and water eat away at four of his toes and his foot for five hours.

At the age of forty-four, he finally hit bottom. And then the miracle happened. He saw a wooden sign with the Serenity Prayer printed on it. He had been to A.A. before, in and out of A.A. in Los Angeles, Phoenix, and San Francisco. He remembered that at one of his first A.A. meetings he had heard, "If you are an alcoholic and if you continue to drink, the end is death or insanity." He added, "They hadn't mentioned the living hell before death."

After seeing that sign, he took the first three Steps for the first time. He surrendered totally. Now he began to sleep, to relax, to accept his plight. He started going to A.A. in prison at the group's next meeting.

While still in prison, Morris was given training and after he was paroled, he went to work as a counselor in Corrections, then worked for a County Mental Health organization, and when he wrote his story had been an alcoholism counselor for over a year and was off parole.

Morris was almost fifty years old when he wrote his story and was expecting soon to meet his ex-wife and his two children, whom he had not seen in twenty-three years. His son was to be married and wanted Morris at the wedding. His ex-wife, from whom he had not heard in over twenty-three years, had telephoned him three weeks earlier about the wedding.

He wrote: "I am still arrogant, egocentric, self-righteous, with no humility, even phony at times, but I'm trying to be a better person and help my fellowmen. Guess I'll never be a saint, but whatever I am, I want to be sober and in A.A."

He ended his story by saying: "God bless all you people in A.A. and especially you fellows in prison. Remember, now you have a choice."

When last heard of Morris was living in North Carolina.

Promoted to Chronic

Helen B., New York

2nd ed. p. 485, 3rd ed. p. 464

"This career girl preferred solitary drinking, the blackout kind, often hoping she'd stay that way for keeps. But Providence had other ideas."

Helen entered A.A. in New York in November of 1944 but had a slip in 1945.

She started drinking socially and at parties and proms when she was about twenty years old. It made her feel quite grownup and mature, and another added attraction was that as far as her family was concerned it was forbidden.

Eventually she became dependent on it and became a daily drinker. Then she had a week-long bender of solitary drinking, locked up a hotel room because her family opposed her coming marriage. During that week the hotel doctor gave her sleeping pills and she took the whole bottle. Only the actions of an alert hotel maid saved her.

The next five years were filled with fear, failure and frustration. Her doctor had suggested to her husband that he send her to A.A. but little was known about it then. The doctor said it was a bunch of drunks who helped one another. Her husband thought the last thing she needed was to be around a bunch of drunks. She lost a child, her marriage ended and she was living with her parents. She was in and out of sanitariums.

One day her psychiatrist left Helen's case history on her desk when she was called away from the room. Helen read it and was delighted to see that "Periodic Drinker" had been crossed out and the words "Chronic Alcoholic" substituted. She thought this mean she was getting better.

Finally, in November of 1944, she went to Alcoholics Anonymous. "A.A. took this wreck of a woman and brought her back to life."

Her sponsor was "a charming, delightful, lovely person," and Helen put her on a pedestal. She centered her life on this woman. Her sponsor recognized that she was depending on her and not on the A.A. program and began to pull away. When the sponsor broke a luncheon date with her, Helen got drunk to punish her. That was February of 1945, and Helen was sent back to the sanitarium in which she had been so often.

While hospitalized, Helen realized that she had not been basing her sobriety on the book, or the group, or the Higher Power, but on an individual. She started really working the program and never drank again.

In December of 1949, Helen became a senior staff member at the New York office, where she recommended Nell Wing to work as Bill's secretary. She had previously worked for the Boston Central Service Office of A.A.

She proved of tremendous help to Bill W., especially in promoting the Traditions and the Conference idea to the Fellowship, and in organizing the General Service Conference. She served as secretary of the first two Conferences. Helen also worked closely with Bill on the booklet called "The Third Legacy." Bill said of her, in *Alcoholics Anonymous Comes of Age*, "Helen B. of the office staff had a real flair for statesmanship in the best sense of the word, and she understood practical politics too. Her assistance throughout proved invaluable."

In March 1955, she resigned to be married, and moved to Texas.

Join the Tribe

Maynard B., Fairfield, Connecticut

3rd ed. p. 474

"From a Canadian reservation to overseas bars to New England lockups, an Indian traveled a long trail that finally led him home to A.A."

This story was first published in the A.A. *Grapevine* in February 1976 as "Son of Tall Man."

Maynard was born on a Maliseet Indian reservation in Canada, the oldest of thirteen children. He apparently was raised as a Christian as he says he was an altar boy at the church on the reservation.

He had his first drink in his early teens. But he was afraid of his father, whom he calls "Tall Man," so he didn't drink much in the beginning. But he thinks he was an alcoholic from the first drink.

When he was twenty-one his cousin came home from the U.S. Army on leave. Maynard stayed with him at his aunt's house in Maine. That night they drank beer at a tavern and his cousin gave him drinks from a bottle of "hard stuff." Maynard had his first blackout.

He joined the Canadian Army but could not run away from his problem. He found that canteens served drinks to Indians in uniform. His heavy drinking and blackouts continued for the next two years.

When he came home his father met him and they drank together. Soon he was getting arrested and to avoid going to jail he kept moving from one place to another. He tried going on the "water wagon" for a few months.

In Connecticut some policemen tried to help him, but soon tired of him and bought him a one-way ticket to Canada, packed his clothes and put him on a train.

He considered suicide but didn't want to cause more pain to his parents. Then he remembered hearing of an Indian who was in A.A. He found him and they talked. He took him to a meeting in a small town in Maine. He did not drink again. He jumped from the first step to the twelfth and tried to help his brother. Two weeks later his brother joined A.A. and stopped drinking.

Eventually he and his brother went back to Canada to carry the message to Tall Man. Two years later Tall Man also got sober and started a group on the reservation.

Tall Man died sober, five years before Maynard wrote his story for the 3d edition. A newsletter reported of Tall Man: "With tireless devotion and humility, this venerable Indian gentleman traveled thousands of miles humbly pleading for sobriety. He planted many seeds, and it will be many moons before another rises to walk in his shoes."

Maynard tells Indians: "Don't be afraid to join A.A. I once hear people say only Indians crazy when drunk. If so, A.A. full of Indians. Join the tribe!"

Belle of the Bar

Author unknown

3rd ed. p. 478

"Waitress by day, barfly by night, she drifted down the years into jail. Then A.A. showed her the beauty of normal living, in a whole family reborn."

This alcoholic woman had been "slinging hash" for eighteen years, and she thought she was managing. She had a beat-up car that wasn't paid for, no clothes, no money, no home, no real friends to speak of, and was mentally and physically pooped, "but I was doing all right!"

She began drinking at the age of twelve and quit at thirty-two. She also had a pill problem and for two years she was also addicted to heroin, using as many as twenty caps a day. She felt she had wasted twenty years of her life but was fortunate not to have brain damage.

After being arrested and serving six months on drug charges she didn't go back to heroin. Her poor mother had "three of her kids in jail that year—two sons and a daughter." A few years later an older brother died in a house fire because of "pills and booze."

She attempted suicide on several occasions "making sure there was always somebody within reaching distance." On one of these occasions her brother-in-law ran to her rescue but she wound up in a mental institution.

Finally, she and her surviving siblings were all in A.A. and her mother in Al-Anon.

In her story she told of the many benefits she had received from A.A. She had a happy marriage to a man she met in A.A. He taught her that in their new life she was the most important person of all. For her, her sobriety came before his or even before her feeling for him. He taught her that she must help herself first, only then would she be able to help others.

She and her husband were aware of the nice things around them, things they had never noticed before in their drunken stupor. She planted her first flower garden the year she wrote her story, and she was enjoying hockey games with her husband and her brother without being "all boozed up." She went to church on Easter Sunday with her husband and "it didn't hurt at all." (And the church walls didn't tumble down.)

She knew that the biggest word for her in A.A. is "honesty." "I don't believe this program would work for me if I didn't get honest with myself about everything. Honesty is the easiest word for me to understand because it is the exact opposite of what I've been doing all my life. Therefore, it will be the hardest to work on. But I will never be totally honest—that would make me perfect and none of us can claim to be perfect. Only God is."

Fiona Dodd, The Big Book Stories

Jim's Story

Jim S., M.D., Washington, D.C.

2nd ed. p. 471, 3rd ed. p. 483

"This physician, the originator of A.A's first black group, but badly caught in the toils, tells of his release and of how freedom came as he worked among his own people."

Jim was born in a small town in Virginia, the son of a country physician. They lived just a few doors from the First Baptist Church and as a small boy Jim would often ask, when they had funerals, whether the person was good or bad and whether they were going to heaven or hell. His mother, recently converted, was something of a religious fanatic. She was very Puritanical and did not allow card playing, although both parents drank moderately.

His father was from the South and had suffered a great deal there. He was a doctor and wanted to give his son the best, and nothing but being a doctor would suffice. Jim never thought he was as good a doctor as his father, whose medical ability was "a gift." His father also had a mail order business since there was not much money in medicine at the time.

Jim attended elementary and high schools in Washington, D.C. and then attended Howard University. His internship was in Washington. Because of his mother's Puritanical training about sex, he married much younger than he might have otherwise. (His mother didn't like his wife, Vi, in part because she had been married before.) They had three children. After they had their first child his parents became allies, but when Jim became an alcoholic they both turned against him.

Jim's real trouble with alcohol began about 1935 during the Great Depression. He had lost practically all his property except the place they were living. He had to give up a lot of things to which he had been accustomed. His wife expressed concern about his drinking so he started lying about it and hiding bottles.

Then in 1940 man whom he had known for years came to his office. He filled a prescription for the man's wife while in a blackout. That frightened him and he talked to a psychiatrist about it, and a minister for whom he had a lot of respect. But nothing seemed to be the answer. He went to work for the Federal Government, while still maintaining evening office hours.

Then he went to North Carolina because they told him the county he was going to was "dry." He managed to stay sober there about six months. Vi had secured work with the government in Washington and did not move to North Carolina, as he had expected. So, he started drinking again. His physical condition deteriorated (he had his first stomach hemorrhage), and he was in financial difficulties, having borrowed money and drunk it all up, so he decided to return to Washington.

His wife received him graciously, although she was living with the children in a one-room apartment. When he struck her with his fist, she got a court order against him and he went back to his mother. Things continued to get worse for Jim until one day, in a blackout, he stabbed Vi with a penknife. Vi testified that he was basically a fine fellow and a good husband, but that he drank too much.

He was committed for thirty days observation. He moved around the country for a time after that but soon went back to Washington.

When repairing an electric outlet for a friend, to earn some drinking money, he met Ella G., whom he had known years before but didn't recognize. Ella arranged for Jim to meet Charlie G., who became his sponsor. Charlie was a white man.

The following Sunday Jim met with Ella, Charlie, and three or four others at Ella's house. "That was the first meeting of a colored group in A.A.," so far as he knew. Soon Jim began looking for a place for them to hold meetings and was finally allowed to use a room at the YMCA at two dollars a night. In the beginning the meetings were often only Jim and Ella, but gradually the group began to grow.

Charlie and many other white members of A.A. came to their meeting and taught them a great deal about how to hold meetings and about Twelve Step work. "Indeed," wrote Jim, "without their help we couldn't possibly have gone on. They saved us endless time and lost motion. And, not only that, but they gave us financial help. Even when we were paying that two dollars a night, they often paid it for us because our collection was so small."

Jim was unemployed at the time and being supported by Vi. So, he devoted all his time to the building of that group. Jim had found this new "something," and wanted to give it to everybody who had a problem. "We didn't save the world, but we did manage to help some individuals," he wrote.

Jim spoke at the "God as We Understand Him" meeting held Sunday morning at the International Convention in St. Louis in 1955. Bill wrote in *A.A. Comes of Age:*

> Deep silence fell as Dr. Jim S., the A.A. speaker, told of his life experience and the serious drinking that led to the crises which had brought about his spiritual awakening. He re-enacted for us his own struggle to start the very first group among Negroes, his own people. Aided by a tireless and eager wife, he had turned his home into a combined hospital and A.A. meeting place, free to all. He told how early failure had finally been transformed under God's grace into amazing success, we who listened realized that A.A., not only could cross seas and mountains and boundaries of language and nation but could surmount obstacles of race and creed as well.

Our Southern Friend

John Henry Fitzhugh (Fitz) M., Cumberstone, Maryland

1st ed. p. 226, 2nd ed. p. 460, 3rd ed. p. 497, 4th ed. p. 208. In the first three editions it appeared in the section "They Nearly Lost All."

> *"Pioneer A.A., minister's son, and southern farmer, he asked, 'Who am I to say there is no God?'"*

Fitz's date of sobriety was October 1935. He was Bill's second success at twelfth stepping after he returned from Akron in 1935. (The first was Hank P., "The Unbeliever" in the 1st edition.)

Fitz has been described as a blue blood from Maryland. Alcoholism may have run in his mother's side of the family. Fitz was reportedly quite handsome, with chiseled features. He had the quiet, easy charm of the landed gentry. Indeed, he was quite the Southern gentleman. Lois W. said Fitz was an impractical, lovable dreamer. His intellectual, scholarly qualities gave him common ground with Bill who—like Fitz—was also a dreamer.

He was the son of an Episcopalian minister. Alcoholism may have run in his mother's side of the family. They never drank at home, but when Fitz took his first drink when at college, he discovered that it removed his fear and sense of inferiority.

He attempted to enlist during World War I but could not pass the physical. This added to his sense of inferiority.

He had a good job with a large corporation until the Great Depression. Later he worked at various jobs: traveling salesman, teacher and farmer. But he couldn't stop drinking. He was drunk when his mother-in-law died, when his own mother died, when his child was born.

His wife had heard of Towns Hospital in New York and urged him to go there. Finally he agreed.

Another patient told him about a group of men who were worse than he was but who didn't drink any more. This patient had tried the program but had slipped. He knew it was because he hadn't been honest. He asked Fitz if he believed in God. Fitz did not. Later, in his bed, the thought came: "Can all the worthwhile people I have known be wrong about God?" He took a look at his own history and suddenly a thought like a Voice came: "Who are you to say there is no God?"

Bill and Lois W. and Fitz M. and his wife became devoted friends and visited one another often. Fitz frequently came up for the Tuesday night meeting at the Wilson home in Brooklyn. It was while Bill and Lois Wilson were visiting Fitz in Maryland in the summer of 1936 that a lawyer and card player named Bill C. committed suicide in Bill and Lois's home (see page 16 of the Big Book). And Fitz, as well as Hank P., often joined Bill and Lois at Oxford Group house parties before A.A. broke away from the Oxford Group.

During the writing of the Big Book, Fitz insisted that the book should express Christian doctrines and use Biblical terms and expressions. Hank and Jim B. opposed him. The compromise was "God as we understood Him."

When the group was trying to decide on a name for the book, Fitz, because of his close proximity to Washington, was asked to go to the Library of Congress and find out how many books were called "The Way Out."

His sister Agnes came to their assistance when the printer refused to release the book he was holding, the first printing of *Alcoholics Anonymous*. Agnes loaned A.A. $1,000, the equivalent of nearly $12,000 today.

Fitz later started A.A. in Washington, D.C. Florence R. ("A Feminine Victory" in the 1st edition) joined him there. It was Fitz who was called on to identify her body when she died. He sent one of his early sponsees (who never recovered) to see his old friend Jim

B. in Washington ("The Vicious Cycle") when Jim was just coming off a binge.

In World War II, Fitz at last was able to join the Army, where he was found to be suffering from cancer. He died October 4, 1943, eight years after he stopped drinking. Fitz is buried on the grounds of Christ Episcopal Church at Owensville, Maryland, where his father had once been pastor. He is buried just a few feet from Jim B.

The Prisoner Freed

Author unknown, New York City

2nd ed. p. 495, 3rd ed. p. 508

"After twenty years in prison for murder, he knew A.A. was the spot for him—if he wanted to stay on the outside."

This alcoholic first heard of A.A. and went to his first meetings when he was in prison. He probably joined the fellowship in 1950 or 1951. He slipped after ten months, but by the time he wrote his story for the second edition he had four years sobriety.

He started drinking when he was about sixteen but had to hide it from his father. After his father died, he "rolled along with the mob" for years until one day, returning from a four-day drunk, a detective was waiting for him. He had shot and killed one person and almost killed a second.

He was indicted for murder in the first degree, and feared he would get the death penalty, but the jury brought back a verdict of murder in the second degree, for which he received a sentence of twenty years to life. He received an additional sentence of fifteen years for attempted murder of the other man. He was sent to Sing expecting to serve a minimum of thirty-five years, as at that time there was no time off for good behavior. Eventually the laws were changed and he was released after serving twenty years and nine months.

During that time he was incarcerated at Sing, at Dannemora in the Adirondacks, and at a place Wallkill, "a so-called rehabilitation center." It was at Wallkill that he first heard of A.A. from two other inmates. He didn't like A.A., but his two friends kept insisting he go back to the meetings.

When he was released from prison, he made excuses to his parole officer for not going to A.A. Then one day he ran into the old crowd and got drunk. His mother was heartbroken and asked if he were going to do this to her all over again.

He told her he would not. He finally joined A.A., and after a slip at ten months stayed sober. His mother was still alive at the age of eighty-two when he wrote his story.

Life was no bed of roses, but when something happened that upset him, instead of walking in and throwing a buck at the barman, he walked into a phone booth and dropped a dime in the box to call an A.A. member.

He considered himself very lucky to have found A.A. and the A.A. program to hang on to and carry him through.

Desperation Drinking

Pat M., New York City

2nd ed. p. 509, 3rd ed. p. 512

"He was drinking to hold on to his job, to hold on to his wife, to hold on to his sanity. Finally, he was drinking to keep away those little men, and those strange voices, and the organ music that came out of the walls."

Pat probably joined AA and stopped drinking about 1952.

He was born in Ireland and came to the United States as a child. He started drinking at the age of sixteen but wasn't a social drinker very long. He had blackouts, began swearing off alcohol, and taking the morning drink quite early. He became a binge drinker.

He thought the Army would be a cure-all, a new life. But when he returned from the Army things were probably worse because now, he had a lot more resentments.

He married the girl he'd left behind, who had been warned by his own mother that he was a hopeless drunk. He stayed sober for her for nine months but then took a drink at a party. No one had warned him that it was the first drink that did the damage. His drinking became desperation drinking.

Finally, he hit bottom. He knew he had come to the end of his rope and turned for help to someone he had turned his back on for years: God. He then went to the doctor who had treated him for DTs. The doctor sent him to the Alanon House on the West Side. There he was introduced to A.A. He found friendship and understanding he needed; he learned how to pray honestly.

Pat didn't take the tenth step inventory at night. He took it continuously during the day. At the time he wrote his story he had not had a drink since his first meeting.

For him, A.A. had become a way of life.

The Career Officer

Sackville O'C. M., Dublin, Ireland

2nd ed. p. 523, 3rd ed. p. 517

"A British officer, this Irishman—that is, until brandy 'retired' him. But this proved only a temporary setback. He survived to become a mainstay of A.A. in Eire."

Sackville attended his first A.A. meeting on April 28, 1947, and never took another drink. He was a "retired" major from the British Army, in which he served for twenty-six years. He had been discharged on medical grounds. This meant, of course, alcoholism. In a talk he gave in Bristol, England, in 1971, he said he received a letter from the Army saying they had accepted his resignation. But he didn't remember having sent it in.

He was living with his parents in Dublin, existing on his retirement pay. His long-suffering mother finally ordered him to pack his bags. He then remembered seeing something about A.A. in the *Evening Mail*, and told her he would try A.A. His parents agreed that if A.A. could help him he could live at home. But he would be on probation. He arrived at his first meeting that night, drunk on gin and doped up on Benzedrine and paraldehyde.

His first meeting was at the Dublin group. It was the first A.A. group in Europe, founded by Conor F. in November of 1946. Conor had got sober in Philadelphia three years earlier and was on vacation in Ireland.

It was known as the First Dublin Group or The Country Shop Group, the name of the restaurant where they met. Sackville found what looked like a large group when he went to his first meeting. But it was the big Monday night open meeting, to explain A.A. to newcomers and their families as well as doctors and social workers.

Getting off to a shaky start, the secretary and a dozen others got drunk in the summer of 1947. Three remained sober, among them Sackville, who had joined in April. They re-formed the group in August with Sackville as secretary.

Sackville was a good organizer who had clear and definite ideas of what they should do. He suggested they switch the open public information meeting from Friday to Monday, the better to catch men coming off a weekend drunk. He also worked hard to get information about A.A. to the newspapers.

Since the vast majority of the Irish population was Roman Catholic, Sackville knew it was important to win the goodwill of the Catholic clergy. He convinced a professor of theology at St. Patrick's College, Maynooth, to publish an article favorable to A.A. in the college paper *The Furrow*. Bill W. later referred to the publication of this article as an impressive step forward in A.A.'s relations with the churches.

Bill W. visited them in 1950 and held a press conference in the Mansion House (the Lord Mayor's house). Many years later Jimmy R. took great pride in showing the kitchen sink in his basement apartment into which Bill had knocked his cigarette ash as they sat around and talked for hours following the press conference. Sackville, in his 1971 talk, spoke of what a great man Bill W. was.

Sackville was a personal friend of Sister Ignatia and corresponded with her and visited her. In a letter to Ignatia in 1959 he speaks of AA "catching fire" in the west of Ireland but of there not being an AA group yet in her native Ballina despite the town's being "highly qualified to support a group of its own." Ignatia presented Sackville with a St. Christopher medal to keep him safe on his motorbike, and in a letter from 1962 he tells her, "Poor St. Christopher, he must find himself very overworked in this country."

In 1948 Sackville began a small paper, *The Road Back*, which did much to give the group a sense of identity. A bi-monthly group newsletter celebrating birthdays and group news, it also carried recovery sharing in a simple unpretentious five-page format. He edited it for more than twenty-eight years.

Sackville updated his story for the March 1968 *Grapevine*. It was titled: "Living the Program In All Our Affairs."

He hoped that what he wrote would not be taken as the view of an Angry Old Man. But he complained of those who give only lip service to the slogans and the steps.

He urged realism, with its frequent reminders of humility, and faith, anchored to some unchanging norm of goodness (God, as I understand him). Also, atonement, patience, and thinking with spiritual discipline.

He complained of those who tell a newcomer that he only has to stay dry for today and to come to meetings. He said the meetings were necessary but would not practice the Steps for anyone. Even the most meeting-minded member has to pass many hours of the day when he is alone and must depend on his own inner strength. These are the hours when practice of these principles in all his affairs must cease to be a conventional, superficial acceptance of them and become a master of the heart and the will.

Sackville also wasn't fond of celebrity speakers. He urged that we take every speaker, silver-tongued or tongue-tied, at his real value of being another alcoholic who is doing his best to stay recovered himself and trying to help us to do the same.

And he thought that the increasing numbers of conventions and the like were diverting time and effort from our primary purpose.

He added, however, that these dislikes of his were "very slight ripples in a sea of contentment."

Sackville died in 1979.

Another Chance

Bertha V., Louisville, Kentucky

3rd ed. p. 526, 4th ed. p. 531

"Poor, black, totally ruled by alcohol, she felt shut away from any life worth living. But when she began a prison sentence, a door opened."

Bertha arrived at A.A.'s doors in April of 1972. She was the daughter of a clergyman but had sunk low because of alcohol. She had served time in prison for killing a man in a blackout. It was in prison that she accepted A.A., having rejected it earlier. She only served three years of a twelve-year sentence.

She was a poor African American woman from an area where there were very few African Americans in A.A. And they didn't get involved much in A.A. activities. She thought some African Americans were afraid to go to other meetings, but she wanted them to know that "there are no color bars in A.A." She talks movingly about how she was not discriminated against in A.A., nor made to feel different in any way.

He Who Loses His Life

E. B. R. (Bob) — New York City

2nd ed. p. 540, 3rd ed. p. 531

"An ambitious playwright, he let his brains get so far ahead of his emotions that he collapsed into suicidal drinking. To learn to live, he nearly died."

Bob, as he calls himself in his story, found A.A. and stopped drinking in January 1947. He wrote an update of his story for the September 1967 A.A. *Grapevine*, which he signed with the initials E. B. R.

He had wanted to be a great author and write plays, but was stuck in a job he hated, with people he disliked. Disappointed with his life, he at first planned to kill himself, but then decided he preferred to drink himself to death. Instead, he drank himself into lost jobs, jails, hospitals, and heavy debt.

At the point he first went to A.A. it had not worked for him, *because he had not worked for A.A.* His serious drinking lasted seven or eight years. After recovery he entered a new field—perhaps alcoholism—in which he taught and about which he published a book. He still wanted to write a fine play.

In his 1967 update he reported:

> The bad old years of suffocating in the deep morass of alcoholism, are years I could have used to good advantage had I not been trapped by this hideous disease. There were seven or eight years before I found A.A.—oh, how I could have used those years! But they were not wasted; they stripped me of everything, including self-respect; but they made me ready for the happiness of the last twenty years in A.A.

Fiona Dodd, The Big Book Stories

Freedom From Bondage

Wynn C. L., California

2nd ed. p. 553, 3rd and 4th eds. p. 544

"Young when she joined, this A.A. believes her serious drinking was the result of even deeper defects. She here tells how she was set free."

Wynn joined A.A. in California in 1947 at age thirty-three.

She was described by the novelist Carolyn See (one of her several stepchildren) as "tall, and with a face that was astonishing in its beauty." She had "translucent skin with a tiny dusting of freckles, Katharine Hepburn cheekbones, bright red hair, and turquoise eyes." She was a "knockout."

She believed that her alcoholism was a symptom of a deeper trouble, and that her mental and emotional difficulties began many years before she began to drink. But AA taught her that she was the result of the way she reacted to what happened to her as a child.

She was born in Florida and, like Bill W. before her, her parents separated when she was a child, and she was sent to live with her grandparents in the Midwest. She reports feeling "lonely, and terrified and hurt." (This common childhood experience may have been one of the reasons for the reported close friendship she had with Bill W.)

She married and divorced four times before finding A.A. The first time she married for financial security; her second husband was a prominent band leader and she sang with his band; her third husband was an Army Captain she married during World War II; her fourth husband was a widower, with several children.

One A.A. friend quipped, when first hearing Wynn's story, that she had always been a cinch for the program, for she had always been interested in mankind, but was just taking them one man at a time.

Sometime after 1955, when her story appeared in the Big Book, she married her fifth husband, George L., another A.A. member. George and Wynn were married for several years and his daughter Caroline lived with them when they were first married. After they were divorced, according to Carolyn, she dated a wealthy insurance executive whom she had hoped to marry.

George and Wynn were a popular team speaking at meetings. "My dad was Wynn's opening act," said Carolyn. "He couldn't help but be funny. Then he would defer to Wynn, whose tale was hair-raising."

Carolyn writes: "Wynn's mother had deserted her in order to go out and live a selfish life. An unloving grandmother reared her in strict poverty. She contracted typhoid fever and hovered between life and death for about ninety days. All her hair and (though she would not admit this) her teeth fell out."

She recovered at about age sixteen. Her beautiful red hair grew back in and she wore dentures "stuck in so firmly that no one saw her without them." According to Caroline, "she began carving out a career as a femme fatale and started drinking to bridge the gap between the grim hash-slinging reality she was born to, and the golden mirage of American romance she yearned for."

Wynn said in her story that she didn't know how to love. Fear of rejection and its ensuring pain were not to be risked. When she found alcohol, it seemed to solve her problems—for a time. But soon things fell apart and jails and hospitals followed. When she wound up in a hospital for detoxification, she began to take stock and realized she had lived with no sense of social obligation or responsibility to her fellow men. She was full of resentments and fears.

When she wrote her story, she had been in A.A. eight years and her life had changed dramatically. She had not had a drink since her first meeting and had not only found a way to live without having a drink, but a way to live without wanting a drink.

Wynn believed she had many spiritual experiences after coming to the program, many that she didn't recognize right away, "For I'm slow to learn and they take many guises."

On the last page of her story Wynn says: "As another great man says, 'The only real freedom a human being can ever know is doing what you ought to do because you want to do it.'" That "great man" may have been Bill W.

Wynn and Jack P. of Los Angeles started more than 80 meetings in hospitals, jails and prisons in Southern California from about 1947 to 1950. Jack P. reports that during this period they were widely criticized by other members of the Fellowship who thought this was not something A.A. should be doing.

"A.A. can be said to have worked for my father and Wynn," wrote Carolyn. "Although they would divorce, neither of them would ever take a drink again."

George died from lung cancer. Wynn, too, suffered from cancer and when first diagnosed became very active in the American Cancer Society.

Carolyn comments about her mother's story:

> Here's the other thing my father wanted, above all else, to write. My first and second husbands wanted above all else, to write. All I ever wanted was to write. But guess who really got to be the writer? Who's the one in our family, who has actually changed, improved, transformed thousands of lives? The woman who wrote 'Freedom from Bondage' under the section 'They Lost Nearly All' in the A.A. Big Book. The girl who lost all her teeth from typhoid when she was in her teens, who slung hash way up into her forties, and who died a cruel death from cancer when she was way too young. She couldn't have done it if she hadn't 'lost nearly all.'

The date of Wynn's death is unknown, but she apparently died in poverty. When her cancer returned, several years after she had divorced George, she contacted Carolyn trying to reach him because she needed financial help. Carolyn tried to persuade her father to help Wynn. When he refused, it upset Carolyn who was genuinely fond of Wynn. Her last words to Carolyn were "I've always loved you," and Carolyn believes she truly did.

A.A. Taught Him to Handle Sobriety

Bob P., Connecticut

3rd ed. p. 554, 4th ed. p. 553

"God willing, we may never again have to deal with drinking, but we have to deal with sobriety every day."

Bob joined A.A. in New York City in 1961, probably never dreaming one day he would be the manager of A.A.'s General Service Office.

Bob was born in Houston, Texas, but raised in Kansas, the only child of loving parents. His parents drank only socially, and his father gave him his first drink—a tiny glass of sherry to celebrate the New Year—when he was thirteen. He immediately saw the effect it had on him and prayed he wouldn't drink any more. But in college he began to drink at fraternity parties and beer busts.

The family moved frequently and Bob found himself in a different school every year until high school, where he was always the new kid who had to prove himself. He retreated into a fantasy world. He became the classic over-achiever and sold his first article to a national magazine while still an undergraduate.

After graduation from college, he moved to New York to pursue a writing career and landed a good job. He was soon regarded as a "boy wonder." But by age twenty-two he was a daily drinker.

He then had difficulty in every aspect of his life. His service in the Navy was marred when he was given a Captain's mast, i.e., discipline for trouble he got into while drinking. His marriage suffered, his values became distorted, and by forty his health was severely damaged.

When the doctor told him he would have to stop drinking he did, for ten months, with no apparent difficulty, but he did not enjoy life without drinking, and soon he was drinking again and his physical condition deteriorated further.

He developed cirrhosis of the liver, had frequent blackouts, severe nosebleeds, and angry bruises which appeared mysteriously all over his body. Despite three episodes of losing large quantities of blood by vomiting and from his rectum, he drank again.

His doctor finally gave up on him and referred him to a psychiatrist in the same suite of offices. "He happened to be, by the grace of God," Bob wrote, "Dr. Harry Tiebout, the psychiatrist who probably knew more about alcoholism than any other in the world." At that time Dr. Tiebout was serving as a nonalcoholic trustee on the General Service Board.

Dr. Tiebout sent him to High Watch to dry out. There he read the Big Book and began his slow road back to health and sanity.

When Bob had been in A.A. only a short time, an old timer told him that A.A. does not teach us how to handle our drinking, but it teaches us how to handle sobriety.

Not only did his health recover, so did his marriage, his relationship with his children, and his performance on his job.

All these things A.A. gave him, but most of all it taught him how to handle sobriety, how to relate to people, how to deal with disappointments and problems. He learned that "the name of the game is not so much to stop drinking as to stay sober."

> God willing, we members of Alcoholics Anonymous may never again have to deal with drinking, but we have to deal with sobriety every day. How do we do it? By learning—through practicing the Twelve Steps and through sharing at meetings—how to cope with the problems that we looked to booze to solve, back in our drinking days.

Bob has served A.A. in many ways. He worked for the G.S.O. for twelve and a half years. He was a director and trustee of the General Service Board for six years and office general manager for a decade. Upon retirement from the G.S.O. in 1986, he took on the task for

G.S.O. of writing an update of A.A.'s history covering the period from the publication of *Alcoholics Anonymous Comes to Age* through its fiftieth year. Unfortunately, this manuscript was never published.

At the 1986 General Service Conference, Bob gave what the 1986 Final Report called "a powerful and inspiring closing talk" titled "Our Greatest Danger: Rigidity." He said:

> If you were to ask me what is the greatest danger facing A.A. today, I would have to answer the growing rigidity—the increasing demand for absolute answers to nit-picking questions; pressure for G.S.O. to 'enforce' our Traditions, screening alcoholics at closed meetings, prohibiting non-Conference approved literature, i.e., 'banning books,' laying more and more rules on groups and members. And in this trend toward rigidity, we are drifting farther and farther away from our co-founders. Bill, in particular, must be spinning in his grave, for he was perhaps the most permissive person I ever met. One of his favorite sayings was "Every group has the right to be wrong."

Bob continued to give his service to A.A. in many ways. At the International Convention in Minneapolis in 2000, he appeared to be handling many jobs. He filled in to lead at least one of the small meetings, "Pioneers in A.A." The program does not list him as the Moderator. He was probably filling in for someone else at the last minute.

He died on January 1, 2008 at the age of ninety.

Fiona Dodd, The Big Book Stories

Printed in Great Britain
by Amazon